LA VIDA VERDE

Plant-Based Mexican Cooking
with Authentic Flavor

JOCELYN RAMIREZ

Chef and Founder of
Todo Verde

PAGE STREET
PUBLISHING CO.

PAGE STREET
PUBLISHING CO.

First published in 2020 by
Page Street Publishing Co.
27 Congress Street, Suite 1511
Salem, MA 01970
www.pagestreetpublishing.com

Distributed by Macmillan, sales in Canada by The Canadian Manda Group.

25   24   8

ISBN-13: 978-1-62414-972-6
ISBN-10: 1-62414-972-3

Library of Congress Control Number: 2019943005

Cover and book design by Kylie Alexander for Page Street Publishing Co.
Photography by Zohra Banon

Printed and bound in the United States

PARA MI ABUELITA EN EL CIELO . . .

Beatriz Del Real Alvarez

CONTENTS

FOREWORD

Jocelyn's new book, *La Vida Verde*, embraces everything I love about vibrant Mexican cuisine, while still embracing the utmost responsibility of a chef in today's culture. A chef must balance the aspects of pleasure with the global realities of health care, environmental sustainability and human and animal rights. As leaders in the food industry, there is no more meaningful contribution that a chef can make than providing resources to households and individuals who desire great food that is prepared in a way that is dually beneficial to their own health and the well-being of the planet.

Her book resonates with me more than any other I have seen in recent years. We both come from a background where we cherish our memories of childhood and the importance of shared meals with family, as well as the influence of those experiences on our work today—and yet, we both have acquired the awareness that, if we can offer something to our guests and readers that will bring more good to the world through better food choices, we are being authentic. Jocelyn's gift to us is that she extracts all of the beauty inherent in Mexican cuisine, and redefines it in the best possible way: that which is plant-based and environmentally conscientious.

Anyone who opens her book will quickly realize that her recipes are inspired not only by experience, but also by a passion to do things differently; to rethink how we interpret good food, yet still provide pleasure with every meal. I have read her introduction several times and always finish with a deep appreciation for her dedication to guiding us toward a communal approach to food and its purposeful sharing. That is the way food is meant to be—a pleasure intrinsic to our human nature, yet without compromising health and the planet that sustains us. Many chefs write cookbooks for themselves or for their peers, while her book is truly meant to guide home cooks toward the experience of her own love for a specific style of food, which clearly resonates with most of us—yet in a refreshed viewpoint.

Jocelyn's recipes have all of the necessary elements for success—beautiful presentation, vibrant color and most importantly, an immediate impact on readers who will have a desire to prepare, taste and enjoy the comfortable, imaginative flavors of Mexico. My personal favorite is her recipe for Queso Fresco (Fresh Cheese [page 26]), which is both unique in its creativity and ultimate simplicity.

I'm extremely proud of my colleague for writing this book. I urge you all to recreate her artistry at home —and I emphasize this, in part, due to the improbability of securing a reservation at the fully occupied restaurants she is sure to open as her star rises.

MATTHEW KENNEY

chef and author of *Plantlab* and *Plant Food*

INTRODUCCIÓN

In Mexican culture, you often hear the phrase "mi casa es tu casa," which means "my home is your home." Growing up, I heard this phrase every time my abuelita opened up her home to family and friends to gather around her kitchen table and eat traditional dishes for lunch. There's something special about being around a table full of guests who keep reaching for the perfect balance of hot and cold stacked perfectly onto a freshly made tortilla as they pass around queso fresco with a bowl of fiery chile de árbol salsa to complement their meal. Mexico has a fascinating history that mixes indigenous, African and European cultures and ingredients, and its people have created some of the most unique and delicious culinary treasures, thanks to that mix of culturas. That taco de queso that guests assembled around my abuelita's kitchen table was an ode to that diverse and delicious history. I saw my abuelita work all those flavors into perfectly balanced dishes that were undeniably magic.

I owe this book and everything I know to her.

I left my career in higher education to start a plant-based food business called Todo Verde using my abuelita's recipes and food knowledge. My mom thought I was insane to leave a good-paying, stable job to start a new business making our family recipes. To her, it seemed as though I was taking a step back from the American dream she worked so hard for by crossing the border and starting from nothing. I saw power in our ancestral traditions and didn't want to lose all of that hard work, which was built over generations. I am using all that I've learned growing up in Los Angeles and all that I've learned from my family to create my own dream that is Mexican, Ecuadorian and American.

In 2015, I started Todo Verde by going to local farmers' markets and making superfood smoothies and agua fresca. I attended a plant-based culinary school to learn more techniques on fermenting creams and cheeses. Todo Verde later evolved into a full catering business with a menu of savory dishes and the superfood smoothies and aguas we've made from the start of this delicious journey. We often partner with schools, churches and nonprofit organizations to host food demonstrations for community members who are curious about plant-based dishes like Tacos de Yaca Carnitas (page 66), Mole Colorado Enmoladas (page 57), Tacos de Yaca Al Pastor (page 61) and so many more that are still culturally relevant. We've gotten such a great response that more people are asking us to do food demonstrations and share recipes with the community.

The goal for this book is to make more plant-based Mexican recipes accessible to home cooks. As generations evolve, we're seeing less home cooking and easier options like takeout and meal kit services. We are making less time for domestic work and more time for career-driven goals. These subtle shifts are helping us advance our dreams, but along the way, we may lose sight of the rich history our elders taught us, which includes the preservation of our food traditions. We share many memorable moments huddled in the kitchen that are beyond the actual food on the table, but that food speaks volumes on who we are. Our food speaks to our history, our cultura. It's important to keep these traditions alive.

Many of our ancestral dishes centered around a plant-forward diet. That changed post colonization, ever evolving our food culture. I invite you to explore the intersection of Mexican cuisine that remembers the connection to the food, land and community and the dishes that have become a part of the culture. Through it all, there is one thing that remains true—nothing says "welcome home" like a fresh, homemade meal made with lots of love.

My Plant-Based Journey

I believe that plant-based Mexican food is both the past and the future of Mexican food culture. It's taken me some time to come to this realization. A few years ago, I would have never imagined myself eating a plant-based diet, let alone being actively involved in the plant-based food movement. It's been a labyrinth of a journey to reach a point where I no longer crave my favorite carnitas spot in LA. Now, this distant, nostalgic memory drives me to master the perfect jackfruit taco piled high on a handmade tortilla and inflated with aromatic steam to let you know it's ready to eat. I was once freaked out by the idea of eating a meal without meat, but I now find a satisfying comfort in recipes that challenge my palate to explore a bit further, like acidic Ceviche de Palmitas (page 21), Pozole Rojo con Yaca y Maíz Amarillo (page 45) or Tacos de Chorizo (page 75) with a punch of umami.

Although there are so many different factors that led to my plant-based journey, the most important reason was the many preventable diseases within my family. Unfortunately, these diseases are all too familiar in low-income communities of color. My dad was diagnosed with diabetes when I was in elementary school—it's a disease that has run in his family for a few generations. Whenever we'd attend a family party and reach for a soda or a piece of cake, he'd always say, "Remember, diabetes is hereditary." While this is true, I believe an unbalanced diet and lifestyle are taught, which in turn creates generational cycles that are difficult to break. I was taught to fear sweets because my parents were trying to look out for my health and well-being. But there are so many other lifestyle-related factors aside from sweets that can cause these issues. Later, other issues like cancer, high blood pressure and thyroid disease made us start to think that enough was enough. It was time to consider that food is, indeed, medicine.

I am now a plant-based chef with roots in Mexico, Ecuador and the United States who creates recipes that still resonate with my family's palate. This book contains some of my favorite recipes influenced by my family and diverse culture. This inspiration comes from the dishes that I grew up eating that were both plant-based and very much animal-based. Recipes like the Queso Fresco (page 26), Flor de Calabaza y Salsa de Frijoles (page 70) or Pipián Rojo con Yaca (page 80) will make you forget that the meat never made it to your plate.

Listen, I'm not sharing these recipes so you stop eating your abuelita's all-time favorite dish filled with queso de Mexico when the opportunity presents itself. I'm just suggesting you not completely rule out the idea of exploring plant-based options. I'm also not trying to convince you to switch to a lifetime menu of vegetable soup and kale salad (or my take on this, which is Sopa de Fideo con Queso Fresco [page 49] and Ensalada de Nopales con Fruta [page 36]). My intention is simply for home cooks to make craveable, plant-based dishes more often.

As you explore the recipes in this book, notice that I do my best to honor the traditional ways of preparing this food, especially the sazón (seasoning). I was recently having a conversation with another chef about our favorite dishes and the ingredients that make them so damn good. We came to an agreement that the things we love to eat are all flavored with plants (herbs and spices), and anything can taste great if you apply the same techniques to a plant-based option. So, I invite you to get a little heavy-handed with your favorite spices, and let your nose guide you as you pull delicious meals together at home with me.

PARA COMPARTIR
To Share

Nothing feels more Mexican than crowding around a table and sharing everything within reach. When we eat, we eat in community. There's always a reason to celebrate: baptisms, quinceñeras, holidays, birthdays, the weekend and parading a statue of la Virgen de Guadalupe around the neighborhood are all good reasons to get together over a menu of shareable plates.

In this chapter, I've tried to capture the flavor of Mexican–American culture in Los Angeles today. The flavors of nostalgia that take you back to my abuelita's table, and the plant-based ingredients that make the process a little faster and equally delicious. Some of these recipes can be prepared as a group, so everyone plays a role in bringing the meal together, just as much as they play a role in devouring it.

Some of my favorite dishes in this chapter are the Ceviche de Palmitas (page 21), the Cóctel de Champiñón (page 22) and the cheeses—it's hard to choose one! These dishes really do take me back to my childhood memories of finding that one last round of cheese my tía brought from Mexico deep in the back of the freezer wrapped in foil, or driving back home from the Port of LA after a satisfying seafood meal with the family. The flavors are just as spot-on as I remember, and I hope they make you feel just as happy.

JÍCAMA Y SALSA DE AGUACATE

(Jicama and Avocado Salsa)

You can find fresh jicama on most street corners across LA. It's sold by street vendors and paired with pineapple, watermelon and coconut with a squeeze of fresh lime and salt. This is a traditional staple across the streets of East Los Angeles that gets you through the sweltering summer months. Many vendors carve out small spaces across the sidewalk to sell the food they know and love best to create economic opportunities for themselves and their families. Their rainbow-colored umbrellas and selection of tacos, pupusas, tortas, tamales, esquites and fresh ripe offerings in bags topped with just the right amount of limón con chile make our city more vibrant and delicious.

For this recipe, our jicama will get the same love it gets from our wonderful street vendors, and we're pairing it with a creamy avocado salsa made with fire-roasted tomatillos, jalapeño and cilantro. We'll use our fresh jicama chips to dip into this luscious salsa de aguacate, because sometimes tortilla chips take a backseat to jicama chips. It's a simple recipe that will take you back to the corner of Soto Street and Cesar Chavez Avenue in Boyle Heights, where it's always a perfect day for street food!

YIELD: 4–6 SERVINGS

For the Jicama Chips

3 lbs (1.4 kg) jicama

Juice of ½ lemon

Pinch of salt

1 tsp Tajín chile powder

Zest of 1 lemon, divided

For the Avocado Salsa

2 medium ripe Hass avocados

2 medium tomatillos, husks removed and fire roasted

½ bunch cilantro

1–2 jalapeños, destemmed (deseeded if too spicy), fire roasted

¼ cup (60 ml) lemon juice

2 tbsp (30 ml) water, plus more if needed

Salt, to taste

To make the jicama chips, wash and peel the jicama by cutting off the root and stem to create a flat surface. Use a knife to peel the papery skin off the jicama, revealing the juicy white flesh. Cut the jicama into ¼-inch (6-mm) slices, then cut the slices down as needed to create pieces that are similar to the size of tortilla chips. Fan the jicama chips decoratively into a bowl and squeeze the lemon juice over the top. Sprinkle a pinch of salt, the chile powder and some of the lemon zest over the jicama to garnish. Retain some of the lemon zest for the salsa.

To make the salsa, add the avocados, fire-roasted tomatillos, cilantro, roasted jalapeños, lemon juice and water to a blender. Add salt to taste, starting with 1 teaspoon, and blend until smooth and creamy. Taste test for salt and acid using a piece of jicama that didn't make the plate, and add more water to loosen the salsa as needed. Garnish the salsa with lemon zest and serve alongside the jicama chips.

ESQUITE CON CREMA

(Grilled Corn and Cream)

When we visited family in Zacatecas, we grilled freshly harvested corn from our family rancho over an open fire. Maíz is an invention created by our Mexican ancestors, and it is one of the most culturally relevant ingredients that has spawned over 6 varieties and more than 500 seed varieties. Nothing compares to the slightly sweet and mostly savory flavor of freshly grilled sweet corn, especially when you add heaps of crema and ground chile California. We'll cut the corn off the cob, and present it family style or in cups—esquite style!

YIELD: 6 SERVINGS

For the Cashew Crema

5 oz (142 g) raw cashew pieces, soaked and drained (see Notes)

½ cup (120 ml) water

2 tbsp (30 ml) lemon juice

Salt, to taste

For the Esquite

6–7 ears corn

¼ cup (60 ml) cooking oil

1 tbsp (8 g) dried chile California powder, plus extra for serving

2 tbsp (30 ml) vegan mayonnaise

Salt, to taste

To make the crema, add the soaked and drained cashew pieces to a blender with the water, lemon juice and salt. Blend until completely smooth to create a creamy consistency. (It should be slightly salty and tangy.) If you have a squeeze bottle available, add the crema to a bottle to decoratively garnish your dish.

To make the esquite, turn a burner on to high heat. Using heatproof tongs, use the open flame to char the corn ears for about 10 to 12 minutes until slightly blackened and blistered on all sides. Hold the corn over the flame and turn evenly until it is charred. Add the cooked corn on the cob to a baking sheet, and allow to cool to the touch. Once the corn is cool enough to touch, use a knife to cut the kernels off the cob.

In a medium saucepan, heat the cooking oil over medium heat. Once the oil is hot, add the chile California powder to slightly toast it in the oil. You should be able to smell the aroma of the chile cooking in the oil. Once the mixture is fragrant (typically 1 minute or less) add the kernels of charred corn to the pan to warm through. Use a spoon to mix the oil and chile mixture into the corn until it is coated. Remove from the heat. Finish the esquite in the pan by adding the vegan mayonnaise and salt to taste. Mix until it's all well incorporated, and serve in a medium dish. Use the crema in the squeeze bottle to gently squeeze on large zigzag shapes over the esquite. If you have some Queso Añejo (page 29) on hand, this would be a great dish to garnish with that salty and tangy finish. Lastly, use up to 1 tablespoon (8 g) of chile California to dust over the top of your dish.

CHEF'S NOTES: Chile California has a mild spice level and slight sweetness. If you can't find chile California, you can use any mild chile powder.

Choose your favorite plant-based mayonnaise brand. I prefer the texture and tang of Trader Joe's Vegan Spread & Dressing.

Cashews should be soaked for 2 to 3 hours if you don't have a high-power blender, and at least 30 minutes in warm water if you do have one.

GORDITAS DE FRIJOLES CON QUESO

(Bean and Cheese Gorditas)

Gorditas are one of the first things I ever remember making as a kid. All the women in my family would gather around a burning hot clay oven or *comal* (an earthenware griddle) in my tía's backyard in Mexico and make what seemed like hundreds of handmade gorditas. Their hands patting small balls of yellow or white corn masa into a perfectly round disk as they caught up on family *chisme* took skill, and it is something I still need to learn to do without having to concentrate so much on my hands.

The masa would sizzle on the hot comal as one of my tías would sit near the comal turning each gordita until it blistered with steam. She would quickly use a small knife to pierce the gordita, and make an incision for whatever we had ready—beans, cheese, meat, potatoes. In this recipe, we'll be stuffing our gorditas with beans and Queso Fresco (page 26) and pairing them with Chile de Árbol y Tomatillo (page 106). It's the perfect dish to make as a group, since there are several moving parts happening at once.

YIELD: 4-6 SERVINGS

For the Beans

¼ cup (60 ml) cooking oil

3 cups (513 g) cooked pinto beans, strained (see Note on page 97)

½ tsp crushed red pepper flakes

½ tsp ground cumin

1 bay leaf

1 cup (240 ml) vegetable broth

Salt and pepper, to taste

For the Gorditas

3 cups (345 g) prepared *masa harina* (for tortillas)

1 tbsp (15 ml) water or cooking oil, if needed

1 cup (135 g) Queso Fresco (page 26)

1 cup (240 ml) Chile de Árbol y Tomatillo (page 106)

To make the beans, preheat a medium pot over medium heat, and coat the bottom of the pot with the oil. Add the cooked pinto beans, crushed red pepper flakes, cumin, bay leaf, vegetable broth, salt and pepper. Allow the beans to simmer for 10 minutes. Remove the bay leaf and use a bean smasher or handheld emulsifier to smash the beans into a rough and slightly runny paste. Taste for seasoning.

To make the gorditas, add the masa harina to a medium bowl. If the masa is too dry and cracks easily, you can add 1 tablespoon (15 ml) of water or oil to massage and knead it. The masa should be moist, but should not stick to your hands. It should be a similar consistency to Play-Doh.

Preheat a comal or griddle over medium heat. Divide the masa into ¼-cup (31-g) balls. You should have 12 balls. Use your hands to press each masa ball into a thick 4-inch (10-cm) round disk, using your fingers to gently press any cracked edges. These will be thicker than tortillas and will take slightly longer to cook. Place each gordita on the comal to cook for about 30 to 45 seconds on the first side. When the first side sears, and the edges start to slightly dry, flip each gordita over to the second side to create a seal and cook for an additional 1 to 2 minutes. Flip the gordita again and cook for an additional 1 to 2 minutes to see if it puffs up with steam. Once they are cool enough to handle, use a small knife to pierce the side edge of the gordita, creating a pocket. Use the knife to make the pocket as large as possible, being careful not to pierce through the top or bottom layer of the gordita. Add a layer of beans to the inside pocket of the gordita. Add a thick slice of Queso Fresco over the beans and top it with the salsa.

GUACAMOLE CON CAMOTE

(Guacamole with Sweet Potato)

Our family home in Los Angeles had a huge avocado tree that produced enough fruit for the entire neighborhood. My abuelito would climb up high into the tree's branches a few times a year, wearing his trusted *huaraches* in order to pick the fruit too high to reach with a fruit picker. Every once in a while we'd run in the house crying for mom because an avocado fell from the tree and landed on our head. It was a risk we were all willing to take for this fruit that became our staple food each season. This recipe honors the avocado with a simple, yet delicious, guacamole recipe. It's definitely a crowd-pleaser you'll want to make next time you have guests over.

YIELD: 4 SERVINGS

For the Pickled Radish

12–14 radishes, Cherry Belle or your favorite variety that is no more than ¾ inch (2 cm) in diameter

1 cup (240 ml) white vinegar

1 cup (240 ml) water

1 tsp whole black peppercorns

1 tsp crushed red pepper flakes

Salt, to taste (it should taste salty)

For the Guacamole

1½ medium Hass avocados

1½ tbsp (22 ml) lemon juice

1 Roma tomato, diced

¼ bunch cilantro, minced

½–1 jalapeño, destemmed (deseeded if too spicy), fire roasted, minced

Salt, to taste

For the Sweet Potato

2 tbsp (30 ml) cooking oil

2 garnet yams, sliced into ¼-inch (6-mm) coins, 16–20 slices

Salt and pepper, to taste

For Serving

¼ cup (4 g) cilantro

To make the pickled radish, use a mandoline to thinly and evenly slice the radishes, and add them to a medium glass jar. Preheat a medium pot over medium heat. Add the vinegar, water, peppercorns, crushed red pepper flakes and salt. Allow the mixture to come to a boil. Once it begins to boil, turn off the heat, and pour the mixture into the jar with the radishes. Cover the jar and allow the radishes to sit in the mixture for a couple of hours before using them for your dish. They will begin to turn a vivid pink.

To make the guacamole, add the avocados to a bowl with the lemon juice. Use the back of a fork or a bean masher to break down the avocado until it turns into a chunky paste. Add the tomato, cilantro, jalapeño and salt and mix until fully incorporated. Taste for salt and set aside.

To make the sweet potato, preheat the oven to 350°F (180°C).

Coat a medium baking sheet with the oil. Add the yams, salt and pepper and hand mix until each piece is coated with oil and seasoning. Spread out the pieces and cook for 20 to 25 minutes, or until golden brown and tender. (Turn the baking sheet halfway through the cooking process if you see that one side of the sheet is cooking faster than the other.) Allow to cool enough to handle, and add to a serving platter.

To assemble your dish, use 2 spoons to scoop and scrape dollops of guacamole on to the top of the yam slices. Each slice will be a different size, so the amount of guacamole per slice will vary. There should be enough guacamole to cover the top of the yam in a neat dollop. Then use a fork or small tongs to add a pickled radish slice to the top of each yam. Lastly, you can finish the dish by garnishing with small cilantro leaves or any microgreens you have on hand.

CEVICHE DE PALMITAS

(Heart of Palm Ceviche)

Growing up in Los Angeles meant eating plenty of seafood. My family would drive down to the Port of San Pedro a few weekends a month to indulge in fresh fish and crab. When I started my plant-based journey, this was one of the hardest things to let go. But this ceviche recipe takes me right back to those fresh flavors.

Mexico is known for fresh seafood and beautiful ceviche dishes, so I knew I had to find a way to create the same flavor. In this version, I'm using heart of palm or palmitas marinated in lemon and olive oil, because it has a core texture similar to crabmeat. The flavor pairs well with juicy tomato, creamy avocado, fresh cucumber and spicy jalapeño to make it a well-rounded flavorful dish. Serve your ceviche with a side of chips or on a tostada, and pair it with a shot of smoky mezcal.

YIELD: 4 SERVINGS

1 (14-oz [400-g]) can heart of palm

½ cup (120 ml) lemon juice

¼ cup (60 ml) olive oil

Salt and pepper, to taste

1 globe tomato, diced

1 Hass avocado, diced

1 Persian cucumber, diced

½ jalapeño, minced

1 bunch cilantro, minced

1 tbsp (9 g) black sesame seeds, to garnish

Tortilla chips or tostadas, to serve

Drain the heart of palm spears in a medium strainer. Slice the palm spears into ¼-inch (6-mm) bite-size slices. (As you slice the heart of palm, some of the pieces will separate into rings.) Add to a medium bowl with the lemon juice, olive oil, salt and pepper to marinate. When adding the salt to taste, start with 1 teaspoon. The marinade may taste slightly salty, but it will balance out once you add the other ingredients. Let the heart of palm marinate in the fridge for about 30 minutes to absorb the flavors.

While the heart of palm marinates, prepare the vegetables and cilantro. Combine the veggies with the marinated heart of palm, reserving some of the cilantro for garnishing. Fold together with a spatula or your hands to incorporate well. (Be careful as the heart of palm is delicate and can break easily.) Add additional salt if needed. Top with black sesame seeds and reserved cilantro, and serve with chips or tostadas.

CÓCTEL DE CHAMPIÑÓN
(Mushroom Cocktail)

Growing up, I traveled through the Riviera Maya in the Yucatán Peninsula several times. It's where our family chose to take a vacation from time to time. Every time we visited, we always made a point to eat at a small restaurant in Cancún's Mercado 28 that had the most memorable blend of acidity and sweetness poured into an ice cream sundae glass. Even in extreme heat and humidity, this restaurant's *cóctel* recipe made you feel like the entire expedition had all been worth the trek.

In this cóctel recipe, we'll marinate minced oyster mushrooms to create a seafood taste and texture that makes you feel like you're in the hot and breezy alleys of Mexico. Pile it high in a glass, serve with tostadas or crackers and pair it with your favorite Mexican beer.

YIELD: 4–6 SERVINGS

1 lb (447 g) oyster mushrooms, minced

½ cup (120 ml) lemon juice

4 cups (960 ml) tomato juice

⅓ cup (80 ml) olive oil

Salt and pepper, to taste

2 Roma tomatoes, diced

1 medium Hass avocado, diced, plus extra slices to garnish

2 Persian cucumbers, sliced into ¼-inch (6-mm) coins using mandoline

1 jalapeño, destemmed (deseeded if too spicy), thinly sliced using mandoline

½ bunch cilantro, minced, reserve some leaves to garnish

Black sesame seeds, to garnish

Tortilla chips, tostadas or crackers, to serve

Mince the oyster mushrooms, and place in a medium bowl with the lemon juice, tomato juice and olive oil. Add salt and pepper to taste, starting with 1 teaspoon of salt. The marinade may taste slightly salty but will balance out once you add the other ingredients. Let the mushrooms marinate in the fridge for about 30 minutes to absorb the flavors.

While the mushrooms marinate, prepare the vegetables and cilantro. Combine the veggies with the marinated mushrooms. Fold together with a spatula to incorporate well. Add additional salt if needed. Top with slices of avocado, black sesame seeds and cilantro for garnish. Serve with chips, tostadas or crackers.

NACHOS

Who doesn't love creamy nacho cheese? I used this cheese recipe to make mac and cheese for a family party a few years ago. My skeptical family members were an angry audience who felt threatened by the idea of changing their beloved cheese sauce for a plant-based version they thought could not compare to the real deal. Not only did they love it—it was their favorite dish!

YIELD: 4 SERVINGS

For the Avocado Pico de Gallo

1 medium Hass avocado, diced

1 large globe tomato, diced

1 jalapeño, destemmed (deseeded if too spicy), minced

½ bunch cilantro, minced

¼ cup (60 ml) lemon juice

Salt, to taste

For the Tortilla Chips

3 cups (720 ml) frying oil

14 (6-inch [15-cm]) stale or dried corn tortillas

Pinch of salt

For the Nacho Queso

3 medium russet potatoes, roughly chopped

1 medium carrot, roughly chopped

Salted water, for cooking

1 cup (145 g) raw cashew pieces, soaked and drained (see Note)

¼ cup (20 g) nutritional yeast

Salt, to taste

For Serving

½ cup (120 ml) Chorizo from Tacos de Chorizo recipe (page 75)

3–4 radishes, Cherry Belle or your favorite variety, cut into ¼-inch (6-mm) batons and soaked

To make the pico de gallo, make sure the avocado is slightly firm to the touch since you want the diced pieces to hold their shape in the pico de gallo. Add the avocado, tomato, jalapeño, cilantro and lemon juice to a medium bowl and gently fold together, adding salt to taste.

To make the tortilla chips, line a medium baking sheet with paper towels. Add the oil to a medium pot. Place the pot on the stove over medium heat. Allow the temperature to rise to 350°F (180°C). Cut the tortillas into 6 wedges. Fry the tortilla wedges for about 2 to 3 minutes in 2 to 3 batches so the temperature stays at 350°F (180°C), and the tortilla chips have space to move in the oil without sticking together. Use a spider (a shallow, wire-mesh basket) to move the tortilla chips, and pull them out of the oil when they are golden and crispy. Place the cooked tortilla chips on the paper towel–lined baking sheet, and season with a pinch of salt.

To make the cheese, add the potatoes and carrot to the medium pot and cover with 2 inches (5 cm) of water and a generous pinch of salt. Bring the water to a boil and cook for 15 to 20 minutes, or until the potatoes and carrots are fork tender. Strain and reserve the water. Add the potatoes, carrots, cashews, nutritional yeast, salt (start with 1 teaspoon) and about 1 cup (240 ml) of the reserved water to a blender. Blend until completely smooth, adding more of the starchy water if the sauce is too thick or chunky. You are looking for nacho cheese consistency that sticks to the back of a spoon and holds a line if you run your finger down the back of the spoon. Add additional salt if needed.

Serve in a family-style dish with the freshly made tortilla chips layered with the queso, avocado pico de gallo and Chorizo (page 75). Garnish with the radish batons.

CHEF'S NOTE: Cashews should be soaked for 2 to 3 hours if you don't have a high-power blender, and at least 30 minutes in warm water if you do have one.

QUESO FRESCO
(Fresh Cheese)

Queso fresco was a main staple I ate growing up. It topped everything from *frijoles de la olla* and *sopa de fideo* to a fresh tortilla with a little bit of salsa *roja*. It's a fresh and moist cheese that can be crumbled over any dish for a light and acidic cheesy flavor. Sometimes I would wake up for a late-night snack and dig into the fridge to warm up a couple of tortillas that I topped with crumbly chunks of moist cheese that *always* hit the spot.

Here, we'll be using cashews and almonds as the base of our cheese that will serve as the perfect punch of creamy, acidic and salty flavors to top many of the dishes featured throughout the book. It's best to make it the day before you plan to use it so it has time to release more flavor.

YIELD: 4–6 SERVINGS

¾ cup (110 g) raw cashew pieces, soaked and drained (see Notes)

¾ cup (107 g) raw peeled almonds, soaked and drained

1¼ cups (300 ml) water

1–2 tbsp (15–30 ml) lemon juice

1 tbsp (2 g) flaky agar or ¾ tsp fine agar

Salt, to taste (it should be slightly salty)

2 acidophilus probiotic capsules

Cheesecloth

Add the cashews, almonds, water, lemon juice, agar flakes and salt to a blender. Blend until completely smooth. Taste for salt and add more as needed. Add the mixture to a medium pot over medium heat. Use a whisk or silicone spatula to stir the mixture until it thickens and the agar fully dissolves. It should be a cream cheese texture. Turn off the heat, add the probiotic powder and discard the capsules. Continue stirring the mixture until it slightly cools. Add the mixture to a bowl lined with cheesecloth, and wrap the cheese with the cloth. Allow the mixture to sit out for 12 to 15 hours, and then put it in the fridge overnight. Remove the cheesecloth and serve.

CHEF'S NOTES: The cashews and almonds should be soaked separately for 2 to 3 hours if you don't have a high-power blender, and for at least 30 minutes in warm water if you do have one. If you can't find peeled almonds, you can use whole almonds with the skin on and peel the skin off of the almonds after soaking them.

Agar is a plant-based gelatin that will help hold all the ingredients into a cheese round.

Probiotic capsules help to create some fermentation so the cheese has a noticeable tang. Probiotics can typically be purchased at your local health food store in the refrigerated section.

QUESO AÑEJO
(Dried Cheese)

Every time an aunt or uncle came back to the States after visiting Zacatecas, the family would get together to exchange the most pungent dried cheese with an orange chile–stained rind. As soon as you opened the suitcase with what always felt like dozens of cheese wheels, the room would immediately be permeated with the scent of my mother's hometown. This cheese is dry and crumbly and adds a salty finish to any dish it's crumbled over as a garnish. I love adding this cheese to guacamole or dishes that have a lot of sauce.

For this recipe, we're going to use almond slivers, cashew pieces and acid from lemons and green olive brine. The color will be a light brown rather than the traditional white, but the flavor will give the same salty finish to any of your favorite dishes.

YIELD: 4–6 SERVINGS

¾ cup (80 g) raw peeled almond slivers (do not soak)

¾ cup (110 g) raw cashew pieces (do not soak)

1½ tbsp (22 ml) lemon juice

1½ tbsp (22 ml) green Manzanilla olive brine or white vinegar

1 tbsp (5 g) nutritional yeast

Salt, to taste (it should be slightly salty)

Cheesecloth

Add the nuts to a food processor and pulse until you get a crumbly dried cheese texture. Add the lemon juice, olive brine or white vinegar, nutritional yeast and salt, to taste. Mix until the ingredients are fully incorporated. Taste for seasoning and add more salt as needed. Add the mixture to a bowl lined with cheesecloth. Wrap the cheese tightly in the cheesecloth to remove excess liquid by squeezing the cheese. Cover and refrigerate for 24 hours. Remove the cheesecloth, crumble and serve.

QUESO QUESADILLA
(Soft Cheese)

Quesadillas are one of Mexico's quintessential snacks. It's so versatile and can be stuffed with anything from roasted veggies, meats, herbs or just cheese. My favorite part of making quesadillas has always been pushing down on a bubbling cheese-filled tortilla with a spatula, making it ooze onto the comal, which created a crispy layer of *chicharrón de queso*. This alone will be the new reason you wake up in the morning.

YIELD: 4–6 SERVINGS

½ cup (65 g) raw cashew pieces, soaked and drained (see Notes)

⅓ cup (80 ml) melted refined coconut oil (see Notes)

¼ cup (30 g) tapioca flour

1 tbsp (5 g) nutritional yeast

1½ cups (360 ml) water, divided

2½ tbsp (5 g) flaky agar or 1¾ (5 g) tsp fine agar

Salt, to taste

2–3 acidophilus probiotic capsules (see Notes)

Tortillas of choice, to serve

Add the cashews, coconut oil, tapioca flour, nutritional yeast and ½ cup (120 ml) of the water to a blender. Blend until completely smooth, stopping to scrape down the sides with a spatula as needed. Set aside.

Add the remaining water and the agar to a small pot. Whisk the mixture until it is fully incorporated, then turn on the heat to medium. Continuously whisk for 5 to 8 minutes, or until the agar fully dissolves and the mixture starts to thicken and bubble. Reduce the heat to low, and add the mixture from the blender to the pot with the agar mixture. Use a small spatula to scrape down the blender and get all of the mixture into the pot. Use the spatula to continue stirring the mixture until everything is fully incorporated.

Add salt to taste, and continue stirring the mixture until it thickens and separates from the pot. It should have a soft dough consistency that holds together. Turn off the heat and mix in the probiotic powder and discard the capsules. Use the spatula to fully incorporate the probiotic powder. Add the mixture to a 6-inch (15-cm) round glass mold and cover with cheesecloth or plastic wrap with holes poked into it. Allow the queso to sit at room temperature and ferment for 15 to 18 hours, until it is tangy and cheesy. Place the queso in the refrigerator for at least 2 hours to fully set.

To make a quesadilla, add slices of the queso to a lightly oiled comal or griddle. Allow it to slightly caramelize, melt and crisp before adding it to a tortilla. For an even more delicious quesadilla, add some chorizo from the Tacos de Chorizo recipe (page 75) or the walnut meat from the Sopes de Nogal con Frijoles recipe (page 83)!

CHEF'S NOTES:
Probiotic capsules help to create some fermentation so the cheese has a noticeable tang. Probiotics can typically be purchased at your local health food store in the refrigerated section.

CHEF'S NOTES: Cashews and almonds should be soaked separately for 2 to 3 hours if you don't have a high-power blender, and for at least 30 minutes in warm water if you do have one.

You'll want to look for refined coconut oil that doesn't have a strong coconut flavor. Agar is a plant-based gelatin that will help hold all the ingredients into a cheese round.

ENSALADAS Y SOPAS

Soups and Salads

When people think of Mexican food, they oftentimes think of carne asada and tacos al pastor as the most popular culturally relevant dishes. I'd like to argue that soup and salad staples have been far more influential in sustaining Mexican people throughout generations. Indigenous communities were not introduced to beef, pork, dairy and oil until post colonization (or "post contact"). Communities in Mexico depended on a mostly plant-based diet of corn, beans, squash, avocado, cactus, tomato and cacao, to name a few. There were some meat options that were eaten from time to time, such as dog, turkey, wild game, fish, birds and salamanders.

In this chapter, we'll explore some traditional ancestral dishes that have been a part of the indigenous cultures of Mexico and have continued to evolve with us to present day. We'll also explore some dishes that have been introduced post contact and how to make them align with ancestral foodways. My favorite dish in this chapter is the Sopa de Fideo con Queso Fresco (page 49) that takes me back to nostalgic days when we would visit my abuelitos in Canoga Park on the weekends. I grew up eating this soup with pasta, but we'll be using Mexican squash noodles to make the same delicious recipe!

LAS TRES HERMANAS EN CHIPOTLE

(Three Sisters Salad in Chipotle)

Many indigenous communities have sustained generations of people with a *milpa* agriculture system also known as the "Three Sisters," which is an intercrop of ancient ingredients: maize, beans and squash. The three are a perfect polyculture that balance nitrogen in the soil, provide shade for the roots and support one another.

Three sisters salad recipes can be as unique as what your palate's dreams are made of . . . with the foundation of corn, beans and squash going in any direction depending on how they're cooked and how you season them. I like to have cooked beans on hand for many recipes throughout the week. If you don't have black beans this week, change them out for any cooked beans you have on hand. You can also use canned beans for this recipe. This dish includes a punch of heat and earthiness with a dressing made of chipotle and oregano to give you a memorable milpa to mesa experience.

YIELD: 4–6 SERVINGS

2 ears corn

1 medium Mexican Calabacita squash or zucchini, cut into ¼-inch (6-mm)-thick slices

1 jalapeño, destemmed (deseeded if too spicy)

2 cups (354 g) strained cooked or canned black beans

¼ cup (60 ml) lemon juice

¼ cup (60 ml) olive oil

1 tbsp (15 ml) chipotle in adobo

1 tsp dried oregano

⅛ tsp ground cumin

¼ tsp crushed red pepper flakes

½ bunch cilantro, minced

Salt and pepper, to taste

Tortilla chips or tostadas, to serve

Crema de Anacardo (page 117), to serve (optional)

Turn a burner to high heat. Using heatproof tongs, hold each ear of corn over the open flame and turn evenly for about 10 to 12 minutes until the corn is fully blackened and cooked through on all sides. Set aside to cool. Pick up each squash piece and cook for 3 to 5 minutes until charred on both sides. Then cook the jalapeño for 5 minutes until charred. Set aside for 10 minutes, or until the veggies are cool to the touch. Cut the corn kernels off the cob, dice the Mexican squash pieces and mince the jalapeño. Add them to a medium bowl with the beans, lemon juice, olive oil, chipotle, oregano, cumin, crushed red pepper flakes, cilantro, salt and pepper. Serve this dish as a starter to your meal with your favorite tortilla chips or on tostadas topped with Crema de Anacardo (page 117)!

CHEF'S NOTES: You can blend the chipotle chiles with the adobo sauce to create a paste to keep in the refrigerator.

If you are cooking dried beans, it's best to let them soak overnight, strain the water and cover in 2 inches (5 cm) of fresh water with bay leaves and salt. Cook the beans until they are tender and creamy, adding more water as needed to keep them submerged.

ENSALADA DE NOPALES CON FRUTA

(Cactus and Seasonal Fruit Salad)

Nopales (cactus) are a huge staple in Mexican dishes, ranging from ensaladas, *guisados* and tacos. Most people either love or hate nopales. They have a distinct tangy flavor that brightens up any dish, but removing the spines off the nopal paddles requires some time and dedication. Thankfully, you can find nopales with spines removed at most Mexican grocery stores. This salad is perfect any time of the year, but I love it best when stone fruit is in season here in Los Angeles. I love adding tangy slices of red Santa Rosa plums to this salad during the summer season. Use your favorite fruit to balance out the earthy nopales, and serve with a glass of Agua Fresca de Tuna con Salvia y Chia (page 143).

YIELD: 4–6 SERVINGS

For the Quinoa

5 oz (142 g) quinoa, rinsed and strained

1 cup (240 ml) water

2 bay leaves

Pinch of salt

2 tbsp (30 ml) cooking oil

For the Dressing

2 tbsp (30 ml) lemon juice

2 tbsp (30 ml) orange juice

¼ cup (60 ml) olive oil

½ tsp crushed red pepper flakes

Salt and pepper, to taste

Tahini (optional)

For the Nopales

6 nopal paddles

1½ cups (270 g) sliced seasonal fruit, such as Santa Rosa plums

¼ bunch cilantro, cut into 1-inch (2.5-cm) sprigs

¼ cup (4 g) microgreens

To make the quinoa, preheat a medium pot over medium heat. Add the quinoa, water, bay leaves, a pinch of salt and the cooking oil. Stir once to make sure all the quinoa grains are submerged in the water, and place the lid slightly ajar over the pot. Cook the quinoa over medium-low heat for about 15 minutes, or until the liquid is absorbed and the quinoa is fluffy. Once the quinoa is cooked through, discard the bay leaves and pour the quinoa onto a medium baking sheet to cool.

To make the dressing, add the lemon juice, orange juice, olive oil, crushed red pepper flakes, salt and pepper to a bowl and whisk together until smooth. Taste it for seasoning, adding any other elements as desired. (Sometimes I like to add a splash of tahini to thicken the dressing and add more body.)

To make the nopales, use a sharp knife, and hold 1 nopal paddle by its stem and scrape off its spines or thorns. Then turn it onto the other side and scrape down its stem until you get to the soft part. Repeat with all of the paddles. Rinse off the nopales, check for any remaining spines and pat dry. Turn a grill or burner to medium-high heat. Using heatproof tongs, use the open flame to grill the nopales until blackened with grill marks and cooked through on both sides, about 10 minutes. Add the cooked nopales to a medium baking sheet lined with paper towels and set aside for 15 minutes, or until they are cool to the touch. Use paper towels to pat down the nopales and to remove any excess liquid.

Cut the nopales into ¼-inch (6-mm) slices, cutting parallel to the stem side of the paddle. If the nopales begin to release any slime, place them back on the baking sheet with new paper towels to drain. Add the nopal slices to a medium bowl with the quinoa and seasonal fruit. Slowly pour the dressing over the salad and use tongs or your hands to gently fold the salad together. Add to a serving platter and garnish with cilantro sprigs and microgreens.

VERDOLAGAS Y FRIJOLES CON ADEREZO DE EPAZOTE

(Purslane and Beans with Epazote Dressing)

Verdolagas, or purslane, is a wild green of the succulent family, and it is considered a weed. It is one of the most nutritious wild plants available and oftentimes prepared in stews or sautéed. The flavor is tangy, slightly acidic and somewhat similar to nopales. They can be eaten raw or cooked down to create a deeper, hearty flavor. For this salad, we'll be using raw verdolaga florets. We'll pick the leaves off the stem for this recipe, but you can reserve the stems to use for another dish. Epazote is an aromatic herb used in many traditional Mexican dishes. We'll use black beans to ground the salad, and epazote, cilantro, lemon and orange juice to brighten the whole dish.

YIELD: 4–6 SERVINGS

For the Dressing

2 tbsp (30 ml) lemon juice

2 tbsp (30 ml) orange juice

¼ cup (60 ml) olive oil

1 tbsp (9 g) toasted pepitas

8 epazote leaves

Salt and pepper, to taste

For the Salad

1 large orange

3 cups (516 g) strained cooked or canned black beans

1 bunch verdolagas florets (see Notes)

¼ bunch cilantro leaves, plus extra to garnish

8 small epazote leaves

2 tbsp (18 g) toasted pepitas

To make the dressing, add the lemon juice, orange juice, olive oil, pepitas, epazote leaves, salt and pepper to a blender. Blend until smooth and taste for seasoning, adding more as needed. Set aside.

To make the salad, cut the top and bottom rind off the orange to reveal the flesh. Set a flat side on a cutting board, and use a small paring knife to remove the entire peel and pith, moving your knife to the sphere shape of the orange. Using your knife, slice segments just inside of each membrane.

Add the beans, verdolaga florets, cilantro leaves, epazote leaves, pepitas and orange wedges to a medium bowl. Pour the dressing over the salad in the bowl. Gently toss the ingredients together until they are all coated in dressing. Taste for seasoning and adjust as needed. Garnish the salad with additional cilantro leaves.

CHEF'S NOTES: If you can't find fresh verdolagas, you can use fresh watercress as a substitute. If you can't find fresh epazote, you can use fresh oregano, mustard greens or coriander as a substitute.

If you are cooking dried beans, it's best to let them soak overnight. Strain the water and cover with 2 inches (5 cm) of fresh water with bay leaves and salt. Cook the beans until they are tender and creamy, adding more water as needed to keep them submerged.

ENSALADA DE "ATÚN" EN CHIPOTLE

(Chipotle "Tuna" Salad)

If you were a latchkey kid like me, you probably ate tons of cups of noodles and canned tuna growing up. These were staples we had in our kitchen pantry that were one step away from an easy after-school snack. A tuna salad with heaps of mayonnaise and a splattering of Tapatío hot sauce was enough to get me through dinner. This version spares the tuna and calls for jackfruit as a substitute. It's loaded with chipotle mayo to give it a burst of flavor and heat and includes kelp and nori for an ocean essence.

YIELD: 4 SERVINGS

2 (20-oz [565-g]) cans young green jackfruit

¼ cup (60 ml) lemon juice

1 tbsp (12 g) kelp granules

½ cup (120 ml) vegan mayonnaise

¼ cup (60 ml) olive oil

1–2 dried chipotle (morita), rehydrated for 10 minutes

Salt and pepper, to taste

2 celery ribs, cut into ¼-inch (6-mm) slices

6 radishes, Cherry Belle or your favorite variety, diced

For Serving

4–6 (6-inch [15-cm]) tostadas

4–6 nori sheets (you can use the prepackaged seaweed snacks)

⅛ cup (30 ml) pickled radish from Guacamole con Camote (page 18)

1 tbsp (9 g) black sesame seeds

2 tbsp (2 g) cilantro

Strain and rinse the jackfruit thoroughly. Squeeze as much liquid as you can from the jackfruit and place it on a cutting board. Remove the non-shreddable core with a knife and reserve. Remove any seedpods from the shreddable parts and reserve. Add the shreddable jackfruit to a medium bowl.

Add the cores and seedpods to a blender with the lemon juice, kelp, vegan mayo, oil, chipotle, salt and pepper, and blend until smooth. Shred the jackfruit in the bowl and pour the thick sauce from the blender over the jackfruit, using a spatula to help get all the sauce into the bowl. Add the celery and radishes to the bowl and mix until everything is fully incorporated and coated in sauce.

To serve, top a tostada with a nori sheet and layer on ½ cup (120 g) of the salad. Garnish with pickled radish (page 18), black sesame seeds and cilantro.

CHEF'S NOTES: Young green jackfruit can typically be purchased in cans or preserved in brine in jars at Asian markets or health food stores.

Choose your favorite plant-based mayonnaise brand. I prefer the texture and tang of Trader Joe's Vegan Spread & Dressing.

POZOLE VERDE CON CHAMPIÑONES Y MAÍZ AZUL

(Green Pozole with Mushrooms and Blue Corn)

Pozole is the Spanish variation of the Nahuatl word, *pozolli*, which translates to "hominy." It is now typically made with chicken or pork meat. This dish was a traditional dish for the Aztecs and only eaten on special occasions for sacred ceremonies. It has come quite a way from its historical origin. Pozole is still mostly served for special occasions, but now those occasions are more like holidays, birthdays and religious celebrations. My family prepared this pozole for my nephew's birthday recently as the veggie option and it got more requests than the pozole rojo with meat option! For this recipe, we'll be using tomatillos to make a tangy green broth, a variety of mushrooms for texture and blue corn hominy along with pickled purple cabbage and radishes for a full range of colors.

YIELD: 4–6 SERVINGS

For the Maize

24 oz (680 g) dried blue nixtamalized corn maize for pozole, rinsed (see Notes on page 44)

Salted water, for cooking

5 cups (1.2 L) vegetable broth

2 bay leaves

1 tsp ground cumin

For the Tomatillo Broth

12–15 medium tomatillos, husks removed and washed

1–2 jalapeños, destemmed (deseeded if too spicy)

2 bunches cilantro

Salt and pepper, to taste

For the Mushrooms

1½ lbs (680 g) mushrooms (oyster, portobello, king oyster), oven roasted

½ cup (120 ml) cooking oil

Salt and pepper, to taste

For the Pickled Cabbage

2 cups (140 g) shredded purple cabbage

½ cup (120 ml) apple cider vinegar

½ cup (120 ml) lemon juice

Pinch of crushed red pepper flakes

Salt, to taste

For Garnishing

½ cup (120 g) pickled radish from Guacamole con Camote (page 18)

3 radishes, Cherry Belle or your favorite variety, thinly sliced using a mandoline

½ cup (8 g) cilantro leaves

5–10 (6-inch [15-cm]) tostadas

2–3 lemons, cut into wedges

(Continued)

To make the maize, place the nixtamalized maize in a pot and cover with 2 inches (5 cm) of water. Allow it to soak overnight. Drain the maize and place it back in the pot and cover with 2 inches (5 cm) of water and 2 tablespoons (30 g) of salt. Turn on the burner to medium heat, and allow the maize to cook until tender and blooming, adding additional water as needed to keep the maize covered in 2 inches (5 cm) of water. This may take up to 2 hours.

While the maize is cooking, make the tomatillo broth. Place the tomatillos and jalapeño on a medium baking sheet, and place it on the top rack of the oven. Turn on the broiler to high and allow the tomatillos and jalapeño to cook for 5 to 10 minutes until they blacken and blister. Once the tops have charred, pull the baking sheet from the oven, flip all the tomatillos and jalapeños, and allow them to char on the other side for another 5 to 10 minutes. Once they're blackened and cooked through, remove them from the oven and add to a blender with the cilantro (stems and all). Blend until smooth and season with salt and pepper.

When the maize is tender, add the vegetable broth, bay leaves and cumin to the pot. Add the tomatillo broth to the pot and stir to incorporate. Taste for salt and pepper and add more as needed. Allow the soup to come to a simmer for 20 minutes over medium-low heat then discard the bay leaves.

To make the mushrooms, preheat the oven to 350°F (180°C). Break down the mushrooms to bite-size pieces, and place them on a medium baking sheet. Coat them in the oil and season with salt and pepper. Roast for 20 to 25 minutes, or until browned and slightly crispy.

To make the pickled cabbage, place the cabbage, vinegar, lemon juice, crushed red pepper flakes and salt in a medium bowl. Use your hands to massage the cabbage until it starts to soften and release its color into the liquid. Set aside until the dish is ready to be plated.

Ladle the soup into individual bowls and garnish with the roasted mushrooms, cabbage, pickled radish, sliced radishes and cilantro leaves. Serve with tostadas and lemon wedges.

CHEF'S NOTES: If you can't find nixtamalized blue maize for pozole, you can purchase the dried maize and nixtamal yourself at home by adding cal (calcium hydroxide). Cal can be purchased at most Mexican grocery stores or online. Add the maize to a nonreactive pot, such as steel or ceramic, and cover in water. Add 2 to 3 tablespoons (30 to 45 g) of cal to the pot, and allow the mixture to come to a low simmer for 30 minutes. Turn off the heat, and allow the mixture to steep for several hours or overnight. Drain the nixtamal maize into a strainer, and rinse several times using your hands to help scrub off the exterior skin off the kernels.

If you can't find blue corn, you can use a yellow or white variety.

POZOLE ROJO CON YACA Y MAÍZ AMARILLO

(Red Pozole with Jackfruit and Yellow Corn)

You can find pozole recipes for soup bases with green, white or red broth: the colors of the Mexican flag. The most common version of pozole calls for a red broth made of toasted chiles. It's so popular that you see this slightly spicy red soup at weddings, baby showers and winter holidays.

My memories of pozole involve the whole family gathering at my abuelita's home in Canoga Park for the winter holidays. There would be a huge pot of bubbling pozole and another with steaming tamales on the stove that would cloud the windows with moisture. There were too many people to count hanging out in the kitchen, living room and backyard waiting for one of the matriarchs in our family to yell, "Ya está la comida (The food is ready)!"

For this pozole rojo recipe, we'll be using mildly spicy guajillo and ancho chiles to make a deep red broth, jackfruit for texture and yellow corn hominy along with green cabbage and radish batons. My dad didn't grow up eating spicy food in Ecuador, so my mom would make him a special batch without the chiles. She would pull out some cooked maize and meat before adding the chile broth so he could join us at the table with a bowl of pozole blanco. If anyone in your family doesn't eat spicy food, you can use this trick too.

YIELD: 4–6 SERVINGS

For the Maize

24 oz (680 g) dried yellow or white nixtamalized corn maize for pozole, rinsed (see Notes on page 44)

Salted water, for cooking

2 cups (480 ml) vegetable broth

1 tbsp (8 g) ground cumin

1 tsp oregano

2 bay leaves

Salt and pepper, to taste

For the Chile Broth

5 guajillo chiles, deseeded and destemmed

5 ancho chiles, deseeded and destemmed

3 cups (720 ml) vegetable broth

For the Jackfruit

3 (20-oz [565-g]) cans young green jackfruit, drained and rinsed

½ cup (120 ml) cooking oil, plus more for cooking as needed

2 tbsp (17 g) cumin

Salt, to taste

For Serving

2 cups (140 g) shredded green cabbage

4 radishes, Cherry Belle or your favorite variety, cut into wedges

½ cup (8 g) cilantro leaves

5–10 (6-inch [15-cm]) tostadas

2–3 lemons, cut into wedges

(Continued)

To make the maize, place the nixtamalized maize in a pot and cover with 2 inches (5 cm) of water. Allow it to soak overnight. Drain the maize and place it back in the pot and cover with 2 inches (5 cm) of water and 2 tablespoons (30 g) of salt. Cook over medium heat until tender and blooming, adding additional water as needed to keep the maize covered in 2 inches (5 cm) of water. This may take up to 2 hours.

While the maize is cooking, make the chile broth. Heat a skillet over medium heat and dry roast the guajillo and ancho chiles for about 1 to 2 minutes until lightly blackened and fragrant. Move the chiles in the hot skillet constantly, so they don't burn. Once they are blackened, add them to a bowl with 3 cups (720 ml) of vegetable broth. Let them rehydrate in the liquid until they are plump and soft to the touch, about 10 minutes. Add the rehydrated chiles to a blender with the rehydrating liquid, and blend until smooth.

Once the maize is tender, add the chile mixture to the pot with the vegetable broth, cumin, oregano, bay leaves, salt and pepper. Stir until the mixture is fully incorporated and allow to simmer on low heat.

To make the jackfruit, squeeze as much liquid as you can from the jackfruit and place on a cutting board. Remove the non-shreddable core with a knife and reserve. Remove any seedpods from the shreddable parts and reserve. Add the shreddable jackfruit to a medium bowl and shred. Mince the cores and seedpods with a knife until they are a similar texture to the shredded jackfruit in the bowl. Add the minced jackfruit to the bowl with the shredded jackfruit along with the cooking oil, cumin and salt. Mix until fully incorporated.

Heat a large skillet over medium heat, and add the jackfruit to the skillet. Cook the jackfruit for 20 to 30 minutes, or until it's seared and brown on all sides. You may need to add more oil as the jackfruit cooks. The skillet should have enough oil to help sear and brown the jackfruit. Add the cooked jackfruit to the pot of simmering pozole, and turn off the heat. Ladle the soup in individual bowls, and garnish with the cabbage, radishes and cilantro leaves. Serve with tostadas and lemon wedges.

CHEF'S NOTES: If you can't find nixtamalized yellow or white maize for pozole, you can purchase the dried maize and nixtamal yourself at home by adding cal (calcium hydroxide). Cal can be purchased at most Mexican grocery stores or online. Add the maize to a nonreactive pot, like stainless steel or ceramic, and cover in water. Add 2 to 3 tablespoons (30 to 45 g) of cal to the pot, and allow the mixture to come to a low simmer for 30 minutes. Turn off the heat, and allow the mixture to steep for several hours or overnight. Drain the nixtamal maize into a strainer, and rinse several times using your hands to help scrub off the exterior skin off the kernels.

Young green jackfruit can typically be purchased in cans or preserved in brine in jars at Asian markets or health food stores.

SOPA DE FIDEO CON QUESO FRESCO

(Mexican Noodle Soup with Fresh Cheese)

My abuelita made us a variety of different dishes over the years, from tamales to pozole, quesadillas, tacos de queso, guisados, *frijoles con nopales* . . . the list goes on. But *this* dish, this was *our* dish. If she knew I was coming over, she'd have my *sopita de fideo* ready on the stove by the time I arrived. My brother, Juan Carlos, loved her chile de *huaje*, and she would have him pick the huaje (river tamarind pods) from her garden when they were in season and make it super spicy just the way he loved it. She knew all our favorite dishes, and it was her way of showing us love.

To this day, *sopa de fideo* and most noodle soup dishes are my ultimate comfort food. There's something really special about slurping up noodles from a steamy bowl of savory magic. In this recipe, we're going to skip the pasta and use julienned Mexican squash in its place with a soup base made from ripe tomatoes and rich vegetable broth. It still gives the soup the same texture and nostalgic flavor and also adds more nutrients. It's the perfect cure for a cold or a chilly winter day.

YIELD: 4 SERVINGS

For the Soup

6 large ripe globe tomatoes

1 cup (240 ml) tomato sauce

4 cloves garlic

2 tbsp (30 ml) cooking oil

1 tbsp (8 g) ground cumin

½ tsp crushed red pepper flakes

2 celery stalks

1 carrot

2 bay leaves

2 cups (480 ml) vegetable broth

Salt and pepper, to taste

6 medium Mexican squash, cut into ⅛-inch (3-mm) julienned strips

4–5 epazote leaves

For the Queso Fresco

1 cup (252 g) extra-firm tofu

1 tbsp (15 ml) apple cider vinegar

1 tbsp (15 ml) lemon juice

Salt, to taste

To make the tomato broth, cut the tomatoes into quarters, and place in a blender with the tomato sauce and garlic cloves. Blend until smooth. Preheat a medium pot over medium heat and coat the bottom with the oil. When the oil is hot, add the tomato mixture to the pot to lightly fry in the oil. When the sauce begins to simmer, add the cumin, crushed red pepper flakes, whole celery stalks, whole carrot, bay leaves, vegetable broth, salt and pepper and cook for 15 to 20 minutes.

Add the squash fideo, or "noodles," to the pot and allow them to come to a simmer over medium-low heat, for 5 to 10 minutes, or until they are tender. Turn off the heat and remove the celery, carrot and bay leaves. Add the epazote leaves.

To make the queso fresco, squeeze all of the liquid out of the tofu using a dish towel and crumble into a bowl. Add the vinegar, lemon juice and salt and mix. Taste for seasoning. To serve, add the soup to bowls and garnish with crumbled queso.

SOPA DE TORTILLA CON CREMA
(Tortilla Soup with Cream)

There are so many different recipes for sopa de tortilla. It's a soup that comes from Mexico City and ranges from broths that are tomato based to those thickened with beans or tortillas. One thing that remains traditional for this soup in any recipe is that it's topped with crispy tortillas. I've seen fried tortillas in all shapes and sizes garnish this dish and no matter the shape, the crunchy bits of fried tortilla offer a delightful texture.

This recipe is a tomato-rich broth base with lots of fire-roasted ingredients for added flavor. The cashew crema added to the soup at the end of cooking also gives the broth a creamy smooth finish.

YIELD: 4 SERVINGS

4–5 medium globe tomatoes

1 jalapeño, destemmed (deseeded if too spicy)

2 medium green bell peppers, destemmed and deseeded

3 medium Mexican squash, cut into ¼-inch (6-mm) slices

1 ear corn

3 dried ancho chiles, washed, destemmed and deseeded

2½ cups (600 ml) vegetable broth

2 tbsp (30 ml) cooking oil

½ tsp ground cumin

2 bay leaves

Salt and pepper, to taste

¼ cup (60 ml) Crema de Anacardo (page 117)

For Serving

½ cup (120 ml) Crema de Anacardo (page 117)

1 medium Hass avocado, sliced

¼ bunch cilantro, minced

8 tortilla chips, per serving

Preheat a cast-iron skillet or griddle over medium heat. Add the whole tomatoes, jalapeño, bell peppers and squash slices and char on all sides, about 10 to 15 minutes.

Turn on a second burner to high heat, and using heatproof tongs, fire roast the corn on all sides for about 10 to 12 minutes until blackened and cooked through. Once all the ingredients are lightly charred, remove them from the heat and allow them to come to room temperature. Once the charred ingredients are cool enough to handle, mince the jalapeño and dice the bell peppers and squash into ¼-inch (6-mm) pieces. Cut the corn kernels off the cob and set these ingredients aside in a bowl.

Preheat a medium pot over medium heat. Add the ancho chiles to the dry pot and toast both sides for 1 to 2 minutes until slightly blackened. Once they are blackened, remove them from the pot and add to a bowl with the vegetable broth to rehydrate, about 10 to 15 minutes. Add the whole roasted tomatoes, rehydrated chiles and the broth used to soak the chiles to a blender. Blend until smooth.

Add the cooking oil to the same pot you used to toast the ancho chiles, and add the jalapeño, squash, bell peppers and corn. Stir for 2 to 3 minutes until all the ingredients are sautéed and warmed through. Add the blended tomato and chile mixture, the remaining broth from rehydrated chiles, cumin, bay leaves, salt and pepper to the pot. Stir once, and place the lid over the pot slightly ajar, and allow all ingredients to simmer on low heat for 15 to 20 minutes. Discard the bay leaves and finish the soup with the Crema de Anacardo (page 117) and mix it in for a creamy consistency.

Ladle the soup into individual bowls and top with Crema de Anacardo, avocado slices, cilantro and tortilla chips.

ENTRADAS
Main Courses

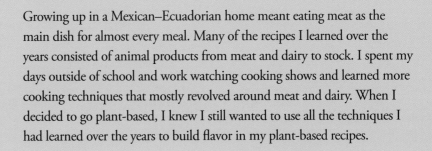

Growing up in a Mexican–Ecuadorian home meant eating meat as the main dish for almost every meal. Many of the recipes I learned over the years consisted of animal products from meat and dairy to stock. I spent my days outside of school and work watching cooking shows and learned more cooking techniques that mostly revolved around meat and dairy. When I decided to go plant-based, I knew I still wanted to use all the techniques I had learned over the years to build flavor in my plant-based recipes.

Most people who choose a plant-based lifestyle, especially people of color, tend to face a lot of obstacles with family and friends who are not supportive of changing the family's "traditional" food. When my dad was diagnosed with cancer for the second time, my family opened up to the idea of considering food as medicine. We were already dealing with other preventable issues like diabetes, high blood pressure, high cholesterol and thyroid issues that are very prominent in low-income communities of color, so my family began to resonate with the idea that the food we were eating may be able to help us heal.

I knew our family had to change what we were eating, and they were ready to explore that journey with me. I started taking over the kitchen at every family gathering, making plant-based versions of the same recipes we had been eating for years. I used traditional techniques to build layers of flavor and really looked to chiles and spices to create a lot more depth. To my surprise—and theirs—we all loved the new versions of these dishes.

In this chapter, we'll be making tacos, chiles rellenos, fajitas, mole, pipián, tamales and so much more. I hope you enjoy these recipes as much as my family and I do!

CHILE RELLENO CON PAPAS, HUITLACOCHE, TEMPEH CHICHARRÓN Y SALSA DE TAMARINDO

(Stuffed Chile with Potato, Huitlacoche, Tempeh Chicharrón and Tamarind Salsa)

Chiles rellenos are one of my all-time favorite dishes because the opportunity to create unique and flavorful options are endless. No matter the choice of chile or distinctive elements you choose to fill them with, they always provide a wow factor when they approach a table of hungry guests.

For this recipe, we'll be using fresh poblano chiles stuffed with roasted potatoes and huitlacoche. Huitlacoche is a Mexican delicacy commonly found in traditional recipes. It's part of the fungi family and grows on the outside of ears of corn. It's hard to find fresh, unless you're in Mexico, so canned, jarred or frozen versions can be purchased at local Mexican grocery stores or online. If you're in a pinch, and need to use a substitute, you can always reach for minced shiitake or portobello mushrooms.

YIELD: 4 SERVINGS

For the Tempeh Chicharrón

¼ cup (60 ml) cooking oil

1 cup (166 g) tempeh, small dice

Salt, to taste (should taste slightly salty)

For the Tamarindo Salsa

1 tbsp (15 ml) cooking oil

1 dried ancho chile, washed, destemmed and deseeded

1 dried guajillo chile, washed, destemmed and deseeded

¾ cup (180 ml) water

2 tbsp (30 ml) seedless tamarind paste

Salt, to taste

For the Cashew Crema

5 oz (142 g) raw cashew pieces, soaked and drained (see Note on page 25)

½ cup (120 ml) water

2 tbsp (30 ml) lemon juice

Salt, to taste

For the Poblano Chiles and Filling

5 poblano chiles (one *always* tears!)

½ cup (120 ml) cooking oil, plus extra

3 medium russet potatoes, diced

Salt and pepper, to taste

¾ cup (185 g) jarred huitlacoche

⅛ tsp ground cumin

½ tsp crushed red pepper flakes

For Serving

Cilantro leaves, microgreens or edible flowers

(Continued)

To make the tempeh chicharrón, preheat a small saucepan over medium heat and add the oil. Once hot, add the diced tempeh and continually mix for about 10 minutes, or until golden brown and crispy. Remove the tempeh and place in a bowl lined with paper towels to gather excess oil. Season immediately with salt. Set aside for garnish.

To make the salsa, preheat a medium saucepan over medium heat. Add the oil and the chiles to panfry for 1 to 2 minutes until slightly blackened on both sides. Place into a small bowl with the water to rehydrate. Place another bowl over the chiles to hold them down into the water. Allow them to soak for about 10 minutes. Check the tamarind paste for seeds and add to a blender. Add the rehydrated chiles, salt and ½ cup (120 ml) of the water from the bowl used to rehydrate the chiles. Blend until smooth, and add more water from the chile soaking water, if necessary, to create a smooth sauce. Set aside for garnish.

To make the cashew crema, add the cashew pieces to a blender with the water, lemon juice and salt. Blend until completely smooth to create a creamy consistency. It should be slightly salty and tangy. Set aside for garnish.

To make the poblano chiles, turn a burner to high heat. Using heatproof tongs, hold each chile over the open flame to char the chiles for about 10 to 15 minutes until fully blackened and blistered on all sides. Be careful to not overcook the chiles. They should still hold their shape and be a vibrant green color under the charred skin. Place into a bowl and cover with plastic wrap to let steam, and set aside for 15 minutes.

Preheat the oven to 350°F (180°C).

While the chiles are cooling, make the filling. Coat a medium baking sheet with the oil. Place the potatoes on the baking sheet. Add salt and pepper to the potatoes to taste, and hand mix until each piece is coated in oil and seasoning. Spread out the pieces, and cook for 20 to 25 minutes, or until golden brown. Allow to cool enough to handle, and add to a bowl.

Coat a saucepan with oil. Add the huitlacoche, cumin, crushed red pepper flakes and a pinch of salt. Allow to come to a simmer, and then add to the roasted potatoes and fold together. Add salt as needed.

Lower the oven temperature to 200°F (95°C). Peel the charred skin on all sides of the chiles and discard. Do not rinse the chiles under water. Use a paring knife to gently make a lengthwise slit down the chiles to remove and discard the seeds. Gently add ¾ cup (53 g) of the filling to each poblano chile, and place on a baking sheet. Cover with foil, and heat the chiles for about 10 to 15 minutes, or until the filling reaches a temperature of 165°F (75°C).

Plate each chile by adding about 3 tablespoons (45 ml) of tamarindo salsa to a dish, and place the filled chile over the salsa. Add a dollop of cashew crema over the top of the chile or use a squeeze bottle to create a zigzag shape over the dish. Garnish with 1 tablespoon (10 g) of crispy tempeh chicharrón sprinkled over the crema. Add a light garnish of cilantro leaves, microgreens or edible flowers.

MOLE COLORADO ENMOLADAS

(Enmoladas with Mole Colorado)

The Nahuatl word for mole is *mōlli*, which means "ground sauce." Mole sauces consist of layering flavors from many ingredients, such as dried chiles, spices, nuts, seeds, fruits and so much more. Some mole recipes can take many hours or even days to prepare. This recipe will take a few hours before it's ready to serve. If you're in the kitchen with a friend or relative, you can split some of the tasks to go a bit faster.

Puebla and Oaxaca are most widely known for their traditional mole recipes, but other states of Mexico create different varieties as well. There are several mole varieties from mole poblano—the most well-known—to mole negro. We will be making Mole Colorado, which has a reddish-brown hue and has incredible amounts of flavor. This batch will make quite a bit of mole. (If you're going to spend the time making it, might as well make enough to last you a while.) You can freeze some for later use or share with friends and family. Use this mole to pair with mushrooms, roasted vegetables, jackfruit or over enmoladas.

YIELD: 6-10 SERVINGS

For the Mole

4 dried ancho chiles

4 dried guajillo chiles

½ cup (70 g) sesame seeds

¾ cup (107 g) almonds

½ cup (65 g) peanuts

2 allspice berries

2 cloves

1 whole Mexican cinnamon stick

1 tsp cumin seeds

4 tbsp (60 ml) cooking oil, divided

½ cup (84 g) raisins

1 plantain, peeled and sliced

1 large globe tomato

½ yellow onion

4 whole cloves garlic

1 tortilla, grilled and charred

2 tbsp (12 g) raw cacao powder

2 tbsp (28 g) raw sugar

5 cups (1.2 L) vegetable broth, plus more for cooking as needed, divided

Salt, to taste

For the Enmoladas

1 lb (447 g) mushrooms, favorite variety

Queso Quesadilla (page 30)

6–10 Tortillas Hechas a Mano (page 98)

Sesame seeds, to garnish

To make the mole, preheat a dry skillet over medium heat. Add the ancho and guajillo chiles to the skillet for about 2 to 3 minutes to toast and slightly blacken on both sides. (Be careful not to burn the chiles; they will become bitter if you do.) Once the chiles become fragrant and start to release a spicy smoke, remove from the heat and place them in a bowl of warm water for 10 minutes, or until rehydrated.

In the same dry skillet, take turns toasting the sesame seeds, almonds and peanuts for 5 to 10 minutes until each are golden brown and aromatic. (You're toasting these one at a time because they have different cooking times.) Pour them into a bowl and set aside. Toast the allspice, cloves, cinnamon and cumin individually until they become aromatic. Place them in the bowl.

Add 2 tablespoons (30 ml) of the oil to the skillet and panfry the raisins for 2 to 3 minutes until golden and slightly crispy. Remove the raisins and add the plantain slices. Cook for 5 to 10 minutes until golden and then remove. Add the whole tomato, onion and garlic to the skillet to char for 5 to 10 minutes until cooked through and soft. Place in the bowl with the toasted nuts.

(Continued)

You will need to blend the mole ingredients in 2 to 3 batches depending on the size of your blender. Add a batch of ingredients to a blender with the tortilla, cacao and sugar, and add 1 to 2 cups (240 to 480 ml) of vegetable broth. Blend until the mixture is smooth. If your blender doesn't break down small pieces, you can pass the mole sauce through a fine mesh strainer.

Once all of the ingredients have been blended, add the remaining oil to the bottom of a pot over medium-low heat. Add the mole to the pot, and add any remaining vegetable broth and salt. As the mole cooks, the flavors will concentrate and meld together, so salt can be added a little at a time. Allow the mole to simmer for 1 hour or longer over low heat so the flavors intensify. Check on the mole often, stirring to make sure it doesn't stick to the bottom and burn. If the mole becomes too thick, you can loosen it with more broth or water.

To assemble the enmoladas, sear or roast the mushrooms in the skillet and set aside. Add slices of Queso Quesadilla to a hot comal or griddle until golden brown on both sides. Add the queso and mushrooms to the tortillas and wrap them with the tortilla opening facing down on the plate. Top the wrapped tortillas with mole sauce and garnish with sesame seeds. Your mole can also be served with mushrooms, jackfruit or any of your favorite vegetables over rice.

TACOS DE YACA AL PASTOR

(Jackfruit Al Pastor Tacos)

Al pastor is a beloved taco filling eaten throughout Mexico and Los Angeles. Although the origin for this taco flavor comes from Mexico, the style of cooking pork meat on a *trompo* or long spit is actually a Lebanese style of cooking lamb shawarma. This cooking method evolved in Mexico using ingredients that were readily available like pork, achiote, citrus and other chiles. For this recipe, we won't need to use a trompo to bring out the deliciously familiar flavors of fragrant al pastor. We'll be using marinated and seared jackfruit to make tacos just as craveable as you might remember.

YIELD: 4–6 SERVINGS

3½ tbsp (52 ml) achiote paste

¼ cup (60 ml) orange juice

¼ cup (60 ml) pineapple juice

3 (20-oz [565-g]) cans young green jackfruit, drained, rinsed, squeezed dry and coarsely chopped

½ cup (120 ml) cooking oil, plus more for cooking as needed

2 tbsp (17 g) ground cumin

½ tsp crushed red pepper flakes

Salt and pepper, to taste

¼ pineapple, diced

Tortillas Hechas a Mano (page 98)

1–2 lemons, cut into wedges

Salsa de Aguacate (page 83)

Add the achiote paste, orange juice and pineapple juice to a blender. Blend until smooth and set aside.

Remove the non-shreddable core from the shreddable part of the jackfruit with a knife. Remove any seedpods from the shreddable parts and add them to the pile of cores. Add the shreddable jackfruit to a medium bowl. Mince the cores and seedpods with a chef's knife until they are a similar texture to the shreddable jackfruit. Shred the jackfruit in the bowl, and add the minced jackfruit. Add the achiote mixture, oil, cumin, crushed red pepper flakes, salt and pepper to the bowl of jackfruit and mix until fully incorporated.

Heat a large skillet over medium heat, and add the jackfruit mixture. Cook for 20 to 30 minutes, or until it is seared and brown on all sides. You may need to add more oil as the jackfruit cooks. The skillet should have enough oil to help sear and brown the jackfruit. Add the diced pineapple to the dish to sear during the last few minutes of cooking. Serve this dish with Tortillas Hechas a Mano, lemon wedges and Salsa de Aguacate.

CHEF'S NOTES: Achiote or annatto is an orange-red seed used to season and add color to food.

Young green jackfruit can typically be purchased in cans or preserved in brine in jars at Asian markets or health food stores.

COLIFLOR Y QUESO
(Cauliflower and Cheese)

Cauliflower is such a versatile ingredient that takes on marinades and spice rubs beautifully. It's delicious simply oven roasted with a little olive oil, salt and pepper, and only gets better and better as you add more seasoning. This dish looks especially beautiful with other color varieties like the purple, orange or green options when they're in season.

This recipe uses a smoky and spicy chipotle rub that creates a delicious depth of flavor that pairs well with this version of nacho cheese. You can use this cheese for everything from dipping to pouring over chips for nachos.

YIELD: 4 SERVINGS

For the Nacho Queso

1 cup (145 g) raw cashew pieces

3 medium russet potatoes, roughly chopped

1 medium carrot, roughly chopped

Salted water, for cooking

¼ cup (20 g) nutritional yeast

Salt, to taste

For the Cauliflower

2 heads cauliflower, cut into 1-inch (2.5-cm) steaks

1 tsp paprika

1 tsp chipotle powder

1 tsp ground cumin

Salt and pepper, to taste

½ cup (120 ml) cooking oil, plus extra

For Serving

Cilantro leaves

Chipotle powder or chile threads

Preheat the oven to 350°F (180°C).

To make the nacho queso, prepare the cashews by soaking them in enough warm water to cover them in 1 inch (2.5 cm) of water. Set them aside for at least 30 minutes to soak, or until you see them plump up and feel them become softer.

Add the potatoes and carrot to a medium pot, and cover with 2 inches (5 cm) of water and a generous pinch of salt. Cook, covered, over high heat until they come to a boil. Once they are fork tender, strain and keep the starchy water for later use. Drain the cashews and transfer to a blender along with the potatoes, carrots, nutritional yeast, salt (start with 1 teaspoon) and about 1 cup (240 ml) of the starchy liquid. Begin to blend, using the blender tamper or stopping your blender to scrape the sides with a spatula as needed. Blend until completely smooth, adding more of the starchy water if the sauce is too thick or chunky. You are looking for a nacho cheese consistency that sticks to the back of a spoon and holds a line if you run your finger down the back of the spoon. Add additional salt if needed.

While the potatoes and carrots are coming to a boil, place the cauliflower steaks on a medium baking sheet. Season with the paprika, chipotle, cumin, salt and pepper, and coat with the oil. Use your hands to massage the seasoning in until the cauliflower is evenly coated. Coat a skillet with oil and place on the stovetop over medium-high heat. Once the oil is hot, sear one side of each cauliflower steak until golden. Place the cauliflower steaks back onto the baking sheet seared side up and add to the oven. Roast for 20 to 25 minutes, turning the baking sheet halfway through if you notice one side of the cauliflower is cooking more than the other. Serve the roasted cauliflower layered over the queso. Garnish with cilantro and a sprinkle of chipotle powder or chile threads.

FAJITAS DE CHAMPIÑONES

(Mushroom Fajitas)

There's something captivating about sitting in a Mexican restaurant when a sizzling fajitas platter moves its way through the dining room. Guests hungrily follow their noses as they turn their heads to see the platter find its way to its chosen eater. I've ordered plenty of those show-stopper platters, and for some reason, I have found that most times, the show outperforms the flavors on the plate. I want to eat the same flavors that I'm smelling as the dish permeates the room, but that hasn't always been the case.

For this recipe, we're going to focus as much on the seasoning and ingredients as we do with the presentation. We're using hand-shredded oyster mushrooms for this recipe, but feel free to use your favorite mushroom variety to make it extra special. I love serving this dish family style out of the same cast-iron skillet I used to cook it to give that same sizzling effect to wow my guests. Hit the skillet with a little lemon juice just before serving, and you'll be sure to turn heads as you make your way to the table.

YIELD: 4 SERVINGS

¼ cup (60 ml) cooking oil, plus more for cooking as needed

¾ lb (340 g) oyster mushrooms, hand shredded

¼ lb (113 g) king oyster mushrooms, cut into bite-size pieces

½ tsp ground cumin

½ tsp mushroom powder

½ tsp oregano

½ tbsp (2 g) crushed red pepper flakes

Salt and pepper, to taste

2 medium bell peppers, cut into ¼-inch (6-mm) batons

3 medium Mexican squash, cut into ¼-inch (6-mm) batons

½ bunch cilantro, minced

2 tbsp (30 ml) lemon juice

1 tbsp (9 g) black sesame seeds, to garnish

3 cilantro sprigs, to garnish

Coat the bottom of a cast-iron skillet with the oil. Preheat over high heat and add the oyster mushrooms, king oyster mushrooms, cumin, mushroom powder, oregano, crushed red pepper flakes, salt and pepper. You may need to sear the mushrooms in batches if your skillet is small and the mushrooms are crowded. Sear the mushrooms for 5 to 10 minutes, and then gently mix in the bell peppers and squash to sear. If you're working in batches, you can remove the mushrooms, and add them back once the bell peppers and squash have seared. Add the cilantro in the last few minutes of cooking when you see the mushrooms, peppers and squash are seared. Taste for salt and add more as needed. Add the lemon juice, sesame seeds and a couple of sprigs of cilantro for garnish just before taking the skillet to the table.

CHEF'S NOTE: If you can't find oyster mushrooms, use any other mushroom variety available, like cremini, portobello or white button, and slice the mushrooms instead of hand shredding.

TACOS DE YACA CARNITAS
(Jackfruit Carnitas Tacos)

Carnitas means "tiny meat" and is a dish native to the state of Michoacán. It's typically prepared in a large *cazuela* where pork meat is braised and simmered for long hours in oil or lard, and is usually showcased as a taco topping with heaps of salsa.

Jackfruit takes on the same shredded texture as pork and has oftentimes been confused as actual meat. I've served tacos at events where guests didn't even realize they were eating a plant-based taco. This dish will call for a good amount of oil to give the jackfruit carnitas a similar texture and flavor. Since jackfruit is a fruit, it doesn't have any fat or oil, so you have to create more richness by adding oil.

YIELD: 4–6 SERVINGS

3 (20-oz [565-g]) cans young green jackfruit, drained, rinsed and squeezed dry

¾ cup (180 ml) cooking oil, plus more for cooking as needed

Juice of 1 large orange, divided

2 tbsp (17 g) ground cumin

1 tbsp (1 g) dried oregano

½ tsp crushed red pepper flakes

Salt and pepper, to taste

Tortillas Hechas a Mano (page 98)

1–2 lemons, cut into wedges

Salsa de Chipotle (page 114)

Remove the non-shreddable core from the shreddable part of the jackfruit with a knife. Remove any seedpods from the shreddable parts and add them to the pile of cores. Add the shreddable jackfruit to a medium bowl. Mince the cores and seedpods with a knife until they are a similar texture to the shreddable jackfruit. Shred the jackfruit in the bowl, and add the minced jackfruit. Add the oil, half of the orange juice, cumin, oregano, crushed red pepper flakes, salt and pepper to the bowl of jackfruit and mix until fully incorporated.

Heat a large skillet over medium heat, and add the jackfruit to the skillet. Cook for 20 to 30 minutes, or until the jackfruit is seared and brown on all sides. You may need to add more oil as the jackfruit cooks. The skillet should have enough oil to help sear and brown the jackfruit. Add the remaining orange juice to the skillet. Serve this dish with Tortillas Hechas a Mano, lemon wedges and Salsa de Chipotle.

CHEF'S NOTE: Young green jackfruit can typically be purchased in cans or preserved in brine in jars at Asian markets or health food stores.

TOSTADAS DE YACA EN CHILE VERDE

(Jackfruit in Green Chile Tostadas)

Tostadas have been a traditional Mexican staple for generations. It is the process of baking, toasting or frying a corn tortilla until it becomes crisp. Before indigenous communities were introduced to oil, tostadas were typically baked or toasted disks topped with beans, stews, cabbage and salsa. For this recipe, we'll be topping tostadas with smashed black beans, jackfruit in a chile verde sauce and Crema de Anacardo (page 117). You can purchase fried tostadas from your local Mexican grocery store, or you can toast the tortillas with a little oil in the oven until they are crisp.

YIELD: 4–6 SERVINGS

For the Jackfruit

3 (20-oz [565-g]) cans young green jackfruit, drained, rinsed and squeezed dry

¾ cup (180 ml) cooking oil, plus more for cooking as needed

2 tbsp (17 g) ground cumin

½ tsp crushed red pepper flakes

Salt and pepper, to taste

For the Chile Verde

8 tomatillos, peeled and washed

1 jalapeño, destemmed (deseeded if too spicy)

1 tsp cumin

½ cup (120 ml) vegetable broth

Salt and pepper, to taste

2 tbsp (30 ml) cooking oil

¼ bunch cilantro, minced

For Serving

12 (6-inch [15-cm]) tostadas

3 cups (735 g) Frijoles Negros (page 97)

Crema de Anacardo (page 117), to garnish

Cilantro, to garnish

To make the jackfruit, remove the non-shreddable core from the shreddable part of the jackfruit with a knife. Remove any seedpods from the shreddable parts and add them to the pile of cores. Add the shreddable jackfruit to a medium bowl. Mince the cores and seedpods with a knife until they are a similar texture to the shreddable jackfruit. Shred the jackfruit in the bowl and add the minced jackfruit. Add the oil, cumin, crushed red pepper flakes, salt and pepper and mix until fully incorporated. Heat a large skillet over medium heat and add the jackfruit. Cook for 20 to 30 minutes, or until it is seared and brown on all sides. You may need to add more oil as the jackfruit cooks. The skillet should have enough oil to help sear and brown the jackfruit.

Prepare the chile verde while the jackfruit is cooking. Preheat a dry skillet over medium heat and add the tomatillos and jalapeño. Cook for 10 to 15 minutes until slightly blackened. Once one side is cooked and charred, use heatproof tongs to flip and cook the other side until the tomatillos and jalapeño deepen in color and cook through. Add the cooked tomatillos and jalapeño to a blender with the cumin, vegetable broth, salt and pepper, and blend until smooth. Coat the bottom of the same skillet with the oil and preheat over medium heat. Once the oil is hot, add the tomatillo salsa. Pour away from you to avoid splattering. Cook the tomatillo salsa until it slightly thickens, deepens in color and starts to simmer. Turn off the heat and add the cilantro.

Add the tomatillo salsa to the jackfruit skillet and mix until fully incorporated. Smear the tostadas with Frijoles Negros, and add the Yaca en Chile Verde over the top. Garnish with Crema de Anacardo and cilantro.

CHILE RELLENO CON QUESO FRESCO, FLOR DE CALABAZA Y SALSA DE FRIJOLES

(Stuffed Chile with Fresh Cheese, Squash Blossom and Bean Salsa)

Chile relleno recipes typically call for fire-roasted poblano chiles that are peeled, stuffed, battered and deep-fried. Although those recipes are delicious, there are so many varieties of chiles that Mexico has to offer! Using dried chiles is not as common, but just as delicious in a very unique way.

I love using dried ancho chiles because their spice level is very mild, they have a slightly sweet flavor reminiscent of raisins and their texture is similar to rehydrated fruit leather. Chile ancho means wide chiles, and it's the dried version of the chile poblano. For this recipe, we'll stuff the chiles with soft Queso Fresco, fresh squash blossom petals and epazote leaves.

YIELD: 4 SERVINGS

For the Beans

1 tbsp (15 ml) cooking oil

1 cup (177 g) cooked pinto beans, strained

Pinch of crushed red pepper flakes

Pinch of ground cumin

1 bay leaf

5 oz (148 ml) vegetable broth

Salt and pepper, to taste

2 epazote leaves

For the Chiles

4–8 dried ancho chiles

2 tbsp (30 ml) cooking oil

1 cup (240 ml) Queso Fresco (page 26)

8 squash blossom petals

8 epazote leaves

To make the beans, coat the bottom of a small pot with the oil and preheat over medium heat. Add the pinto beans, crushed red pepper flakes, cumin, bay leaf, vegetable broth, salt and pepper. Allow the beans to simmer for 10 to 15 minutes. Remove the bay leaf, and use a bean smasher or handheld emulsifier to smash the beans into a rough and slightly runny salsa consistency. Add the epazote leaves. Taste for seasoning, and add more as needed.

To make the chiles, rinse the ancho chiles to remove any dust or dirt. Add oil to the bottom of a skillet and turn on to medium heat. Once the oil is hot, add the dried chiles and cook for 1 minute or less per side. They should slightly darken and blister, but be careful not to burn them as they will become bitter. Add the chiles to a bowl and cover with hot water for 10 minutes, or until rehydrated. You can use a bowl to weigh down the chiles so they are fully submerged. Once the chiles are soft, use a paring knife to gently make a lengthwise slit down the chiles to remove and discard the seeds. Gently stuff the chiles with Queso Fresco, squash blossom petals and small epazote leaves. Serve the chiles over the bean salsa.

CHEF'S NOTE: If you are cooking dried beans, it's best to let them soak overnight. Strain the water and cover with 2 inches (5 cm) of fresh water with bay leaves and salt. Cook the beans until they are tender and creamy, adding more water as needed to keep them submerged.

TAMAL NEGRO CON YACA EN CHILE ROJO

(Black Tamales with Jackfruit in Red Chile)

Tamales have been an essential food in my family for as long as I remember. Tamales de Zacatecas are generally on the small side and filled with a thin layer of guisado or stew typically consisting of meat in a sauce. My favorite way to eat tamales, aside from when they are freshly prepared and slightly fluffy, is when reheating the tamales on the comal sometimes without the exterior corn husk, creating a crispy texture on the masa. For this recipe, we're making a guisado using jackfruit in chile rojo for added flavor and color contrast. I love serving them in the corn husk for presentation.

YIELD: 4–6 SERVINGS

For the Corn Husks

24 dried corn husks

Warm water

For the Jackfruit

3 (20-oz [565-g]) cans young green jackfruit, drained, rinsed and squeezed dry

¾ cup (180 ml) cooking oil, plus more for cooking as needed

2 tbsp (17 g) ground cumin

½ tsp crushed red pepper flakes

Salt and pepper, to taste

For the Chile Rojo

4 dried guajillo chiles, destemmed and deseeded

4 dried ancho or pasilla chiles, destemmed and deseeded

3 cups (720 ml) vegetable broth

Salt and pepper, to taste

For the Masa

3 cups (345 g) masa harina

2 cups (480 ml) hot water

1 cup (240 ml) melted refined coconut oil (with no scent or coconut flavor)

4 tbsp (57 g) softened vegan butter

2 tsp (9 g) baking powder

1 cup (240 ml) vegetable broth

1½ tbsp (8 g) activated charcoal powder (optional)

Salt, to taste

For Serving

Crema de Anacardo (page 117)

Ground chile California powder

Chile threads (optional)

To prepare the corn husks, immerse them in a large bowl or bucket of warm water, using a plate or bowl to hold them below water level, if needed. The corn husks should soak for at least 30 minutes, but 3 hours to overnight is best.

(Continued)

To make the jackfruit, remove the non-shreddable core from the shreddable part of the jackfruit with a knife. Remove any seedpods from the shreddable parts and add them to the pile of cores. Add the shreddable jackfruit to a medium bowl. Mince the cores and seedpods with a knife until they are a similar texture to the shreddable jackfruit. Shred the jackfruit in the bowl and add the minced jackfruit. Add the oil, cumin, crushed red pepper flakes, salt and pepper to taste to the bowl of jackfruit and mix until fully incorporated. Heat a large skillet over medium heat and add the jackfruit. Cook for 20 to 30 minutes, or until it is seared and brown on all sides. You may need to add more oil as the jackfruit cooks. The skillet should have enough oil to help sear and brown the jackfruit. Remove from the heat and set the skillet aside.

While the jackfruit is cooking, prepare the ingredients for the chile rojo. Preheat a dry skillet over medium heat and add the guajillo and ancho chiles. Cook for about 2 to 3 minutes until slightly blackened. Once one side is cooked and charred, use heatproof tongs to flip and cook the other side until the chiles deepen in color, about 1 minute per side. They will become aromatic and will release a slightly spicy smoke. Add the cooked chiles to a bowl with the vegetable broth to rehydrate for about 10 minutes. Use another bowl to fully submerge the chiles in the liquid if needed.

Add the rehydrated chiles, 2 cups (480 ml) of the vegetable broth used for soaking, salt and pepper to a blender and blend until smooth. Use more of the vegetable broth to loosen the sauce, as needed. It should be a slightly thick sauce that can coat the back of a spoon. Add the sauce to the jackfruit skillet and mix until fully incorporated. Allow the mixture to simmer for 10 minutes. If it thickens too much, you can use more of the vegetable broth used to rehydrate the chiles to loosen the sauce slightly.

To make the masa, add the dry masa harina to a large bowl, and slowly pour in the hot water. Mix with a silicone spatula to incorporate the water. Add the coconut oil, vegan butter, baking powder and vegetable broth. Mix until all of the ingredients are fully incorporated and create a loose masa. Add the charcoal and salt and mix until fully incorporated and the masa is completely black. Let the masa rest at room temperature for 30 minutes.

Remove the soaked corn husks from the water once they are pliable and soft to the touch and pat them dry with a towel. Smear 4 to 5 tablespoons (60 to 78 g) of masa on the edge of the wider end of each corn husk. You can use one large corn husk per tamale or 2 smaller husks stacked slightly side by side to create a larger surface. You should create a square of masa with 2 inches (5 cm) of corn husk on both sides. Add 2 to 3 tablespoons (33 to 52 g) of jackfruit in chile rojo over the top of the masa just off center to the left. To fold the tamales, start by folding the right side of the husk over the tamale. The filling should now be covered with masa. Then fold the left side of the husk over the right. Fold the narrow point of the husk towards the folded husks. If you have leftover husks, you can tear them into lengthwise strips to tie each tamale.

Add 1 to 2 inches (2.5 to 5 cm) of water to a large pot. Add a pot steamer to the bottom of the pot, so the tamales do not touch the water. Turn to medium-high heat and allow to simmer. Add the tamales to the steamer with the open ends facing up. Start by standing them around the edge of the pot, and then add the remaining tamales to the center of the pot. Cover the pot, and steam the tamales for 45 minutes, or until the masa is cooked through and fluffy. When serving, open the corn husk to reveal the tamale, and garnish with Crema de Anacardo and a sprinkle of chile California powder or (if desired) chile threads.

TACOS DE CHORIZO
(Chorizo Tacos)

Chorizo is a spiced sausage typically made using beef or pork. It originated in Europe where chorizo is fermented, cured and smoked, making it a sliceable sausage. In Mexico, chorizo was first made with chiles and available spices. It is slightly spicier than the European versions and is made from ground meat, making it crumbly and soft. It is as beloved in Mexico as bacon is in the United States, and most widely eaten during breakfast, although many taquerias offer tacos de chorizo any time of the day.

For this recipe, we'll be using marinated tofu, tempeh and mushrooms to create the same crumbly texture of Mexican chorizo. The recipe for the marinade remains the same as the meat version, so we'll have all the deep flavors of the chiles and spices. I like to top these tacos with a little citrus-pickled onion for crunch and brightness.

YIELD: 4–6 SERVINGS

For the Citrus-Pickled Onion

1 large red onion, thinly sliced

½ cup (120 ml) lemon juice

¼ cup (60 ml) apple cider vinegar

½ cup (120 ml) white vinegar

1 lemon, thinly sliced

½ tsp dried oregano

½ tsp crushed red pepper flakes

2 bay leaves

1 tbsp (13 g) salt

Pinch of pepper

For the Chorizo

2 cups (500 g) extra-firm tofu, drained and squeezed dry

3 dried guajillo chiles, destemmed and deseeded

3 dried árbol chiles, destemmed and deseeded

2 dried ancho chiles, destemmed and deseeded

1 tbsp (1 g) dried oregano

2 tbsp (16 g) paprika

3 whole cloves

1 tsp ground cumin

½ tsp ground coriander

½ tsp ground Mexican cinnamon

1 tbsp (15 ml) liquid aminos

1 tbsp (15 ml) apple cider vinegar

Salt and pepper, to taste

½ cup (120 ml) cooking oil, plus more for cooking as needed

8 oz (226 g) cremini mushrooms, minced

1 cup (166 g) crumbled tempeh

1 tsp dried mushroom powder

For Serving

Tortillas Hechas a Mano (page 98)

To make the citrus-pickled onion, add to a bowl the onion, lemon juice, apple cider vinegar, white vinegar, lemon slices, oregano, crushed red pepper flakes, bay leaves, salt and pepper and mix. Allow the flavors to meld together and the onion to soften for about 30 minutes.

(Continued)

To make the chorizo, crumble the tofu in a bowl and set aside. Preheat a dry skillet over medium heat. Add the chiles to toast and slightly blacken for about 2 to 3 minutes. Use heatproof tongs to continuously flip and move the chiles to make sure they don't burn. The árbol chile should toast a lot faster than the other chiles for about 1 to 2 minutes. Once the chiles are charred, add them to a bowl of warm water. Use another bowl to push them down and submerge them into the water until they rehydrate, about 10 minutes.

In the same dry skillet, add the oregano, paprika, cloves, cumin, coriander and cinnamon to toast until the spices become aromatic for 1 to 2 minutes. Add the toasted spices to a blender with the liquid aminos, apple cider vinegar, the rehydrated chiles and ½ cup (120 ml) of the rehydrating liquid. Blend until smooth, adding more of the rehydrating liquid as needed to get a thick creamy paste consistency. Season with salt and pepper and set aside.

Coat the bottom of a skillet with oil and preheat over medium heat. Add the mushrooms and tempeh with a pinch of salt and the mushroom powder. Sear the mixture for 10 minutes, or until it is crispy and slightly crunchy. Add half of the chile paste to the skillet and mix until the mushrooms and tempeh are fully coated. Let the mixture cook over low heat for 10 minutes.

Add the other half of the chile paste to the bowl of tofu and mix to incorporate. Coat the bottom of another skillet with oil and preheat over medium heat. Add the tofu mixture to the pan. Stir to cook and lightly crisp the tofu, adding more oil as needed for about 10 minutes. Add the mushroom mixture to the tofu pan, and continue cooking, adding more cooking oil to crisp the mixture. Serve on Tortillas Hechas a Mano topped with the pickled onion.

PISTACHO PIPIÁN VERDE CON YACA

(Jackfruit in Green Pistachio Pipián)

Pipián verde is sometimes confused with mole verde. Both typically call for tomatillos, but mole verde has many fresh ingredients while pipián verde typically calls for pepitas. My family recipe does not call for tomatillos, but you're welcome to include them. This simple recipe consists of fresh fire-roasted chiles, toasted pepitas, pistachios and broth. It has a slightly creamy consistency from the seeds and nuts.

YIELD: 4 SERVINGS

For the Jackfruit

3 (20-oz [565-g]) cans young green jackfruit, drained, rinsed and squeezed dry

¼ cup (60 ml) orange juice

2 tbsp (30 ml) lemon juice

1½ tbsp (13 g) ground cumin

¾ tsp crushed red pepper flakes

⅓ cup (80 ml) cooking oil, plus more for cooking as needed

Salt and pepper, to taste

For the Pipián Sauce

2 tbsp (18 g) pepitas

2 tbsp (20 g) pistachios

2 poblano chiles

1–2 jalapeños, destemmed (deveined if too spicy)

1 cup (240 ml) vegetable broth, plus more for cooking as needed

Salt, to taste

For Serving

Arroz Mexicano (page 94) or Tortillas Hechas a Mano (page 98)

Crema de Anacardo (page 117)

Cilantro leaves, to garnish

Pistachio shavings, to garnish

To make the jackfruit, remove the non-shreddable core from the shreddable part of the jackfruit with a knife. Remove any seedpods from the shreddable parts and add them to the pile of cores. Add the shreddable jackfruit to a medium bowl. Mince the cores and seedpods with a knife until they are a similar texture to the shreddable jackfruit. Shred the jackfruit in the bowl and add the minced jackfruit. Add the orange juice, lemon juice, cumin, crushed red pepper flakes, oil, salt and pepper to the bowl and mix until fully incorporated. Heat a large skillet over medium heat and add the jackfruit. Cook for 20 to 30 minutes, or until it is seared and brown on all sides. You may need to add more oil as the jackfruit cooks.

To make the pipián sauce, preheat a dry sauté pan over medium heat. Add the pepitas and stir continuously for 4 to 5 minutes until they are evenly toasted and slightly inflated. Remove the toasted pepitas from the pan and add the pistachios. Toast the pistachios until they are aromatic and toasted on all sides, for 4 to 5 minutes. Remove the pistachios from the pan and set aside with the pepitas.

Turn a burner to high heat. Using heatproof tongs, hold each poblano chile and jalapeño over the flame to char for 10 to 15 minutes until fully blackened and blistered on all sides. Use a paring knife to gently make a slit down the poblano chiles to remove and discard the seeds and stem. Add the chiles to a blender with the toasted pepitas and pistachios (reserve a few for garnish), vegetable broth and salt. Blend until the mixture is smooth, and add additional broth as necessary to create a smooth sauce consistency.

Serve the jackfruit over Arroz Mexicano or on Tortillas Hechas a Mano, and top with the pipián sauce and Crema de Anacardo. Garnish with cilantro and toasted pistachio shavings.

PIPIÁN ROJO CON YACA

(Jackfruit in Red Pipián)

Pipián is a traditional Mexican sauce that is eaten in Central Southern regions or states of Mexico. It consists mostly of pepitas and guajillo chiles for the red version, and all-fresh green chiles for the green version. In my mother's hometown of Monte Escobedo, Zacatecas, pipián rojo is one of the traditional dishes served for special occasions. Like other moles or sauces, it is most frequently served over chicken as a main dish. Our family recipe doesn't use tomatoes, which I didn't include in this recipe, but if you're seeking more tanginess, you can add a couple of fire-roasted tomatoes.

In this recipe, we'll be making a rich pipián sauce that will pair with seared jackfruit for a hearty and delicious main dish. It's hard to find pipián on menus at Mexican restaurants, so it's a treat when you have it at home.

YIELD: 4 SERVINGS

For the Jackfruit

2 (20-oz [565-g]) cans young green jackfruit, drained, rinsed and squeezed dry

2 tbsp (17 g) ground cumin

¾ tsp crushed red pepper flakes

⅓ cup (80 ml) cooking oil

Salt and pepper, to taste

For the Pipián Sauce

½ cup (65 g) pepitas

1 tbsp (15 ml) cooking oil

2 whole cloves garlic

¼ yellow onion, peeled

6 guajillo chiles, destemmed and deseeded

2 cups (480 ml) vegetable broth

Salt, to taste

For Serving

Arroz con Cilantro (page 93)

Cilantro sprigs, to garnish

To make the jackfruit, remove the non-shreddable core from the shreddable part of the jackfruit with a knife. Remove any seedpods from the shreddable parts and add them to the pile of cores. Add the shreddable jackfruit to a medium bowl. Mince the cores and seedpods with a knife until they are a similar texture to the shreddable jackfruit. Shred the jackfruit in the bowl and add the minced jackfruit. Add the cumin, crushed red pepper flakes, oil, salt and pepper to the bowl and mix until fully incorporated. Heat a large skillet over medium heat and add the jackfruit. Cook for 20 to 30 minutes, or until it is seared and brown on all sides. You may need to add more oil as the jackfruit cooks. The skillet should have enough oil to help sear and brown the jackfruit.

For the pipián sauce, preheat a dry sauté pan over medium heat. Add the pepitas to the pan and stir continuously for 4 to 5 minutes until they are evenly toasted and slightly inflated. Remove the seeds from the pan and set aside.

Coat the bottom of the same hot pan with the oil, and add the garlic cloves, onion and guajillo chiles to panfry until slightly blackened on both sides. The chiles will cook much faster than the garlic and onion. Once the chiles are blackened and fragrant, place them into a mixing bowl with vegetable broth to rehydrate for about 10 minutes. Place another mixing bowl over the chiles to keep them submerged.

Add the rehydrated chiles, roasted garlic, roasted onion, toasted pepitas (reserve a few for garnish), salt and the retained vegetable broth to a blender. Blend until the mixture is smooth, and add additional broth or water necessary to create a smooth sauce consistency that coats the back of a spoon. If the sauce is too thick, you can add more of the rehydrating liquid, and if it is too thin, you can blend and add a cooked and slightly charred tortilla.

Add the sauce to the skillet with the jackfruit. Mix until the pipián fully coats the jackfruit and warms through. Serve with Arroz con Cilantro, and top with the reserved toasted pepitas and sprigs of cilantro.

SOPES DE NOGAL CON FRIJOLES
(Walnut and Bean Sopes)

Nogales, or walnuts, are mostly used in the traditional dish of Puebla, *chile relleno en nogada*, where each chile goes through the extensive and time-consuming process of being fire-roasted, peeled, stuffed, battered, fried and eventually topped with a white walnut sauce. If you search for walnuts and Mexican recipes, only recipes for chiles rellenos by the hundreds appear. It may leave the impression that we don't use walnuts for anything else!

In this recipe, we'll be using ground walnuts in a completely different recipe. Walnuts will be used as a ground meat alternative that has a rich and savory umami flavor with ingredients like sun-dried tomatoes, liquid aminos and spices. We'll use our walnut meat to top a sope and finish the dish with a bright avocado salsa.

YIELD: 4–6 SERVINGS

For the Walnut Meat

3 cups (360 g) raw walnuts

½ cup (27 g) sun-dried tomatoes

2 tbsp (30 ml) liquid aminos or soy sauce

1 tbsp (14 g) raw sugar

1 tbsp (8 g) cumin

1 tbsp (8 g) paprika

1 tsp crushed red pepper flakes

1 tsp nutritional yeast

3 cloves garlic, peeled

½ cup (120 ml) cooking oil, plus 2 tbsp (30 ml)

Salt, to taste

For the Beans

¼ cup (60 ml) cooking oil

3 cups (530 g) cooked mayocoba beans, strained

½ tsp crushed red pepper flakes

½ tsp ground cumin

1 bay leaf

1 cup (240 ml) vegetable broth

Salt and pepper, to taste

For the Sopes

3 cups (345 g) prepared masa harina

For the Avocado Salsa

3 large tomatillos, fire roasted

1 jalapeño, destemmed (deseeded if too spicy), fire roasted

1–2 tbsp (15–30 ml) lemon juice

⅛ tsp ground cumin

½ medium Hass avocado

¼ bunch cilantro

Salt, to taste

For Serving

Queso Añejo (page 29)

Cilantro

(Continued)

To make the walnut meat, use a food processor to break down the walnuts to small pieces similar to the size of ground beef pieces. If you don't have a food processor, you can use a blender and blend the walnuts 1 cup (120 g) at a time. Add the ground walnuts to a bowl and set aside.

Place the sun-dried tomatoes in a bowl of warm water for 10 minutes, or until rehydrated. In the blender, place the rehydrated sun-dried tomatoes (reserve the hydrating water), liquid aminos, sugar, cumin, paprika, red pepper flakes, nutritional yeast, garlic, ½ cup (120 ml) of the oil, ½ cup (120 ml) of the water used to rehydrate the sun-dried tomatoes and salt. Blend until completely smooth and add the mixture to the bowl of ground walnuts. Mix until the walnuts are fully incorporated.

Coat the bottom of a sauté pan with 2 tablespoons (30 ml) of oil, and preheat over medium heat. When the oil is hot, add the walnut mixture to the pan. Sauté for 15 to 20 minutes, or until the mixture slightly darkens, the walnut pieces soften and the flavors meld together. Taste for seasoning, adding more as needed. Set the walnut meat aside.

To make the beans, coat the bottom of a medium pot with the oil. Preheat the oil over medium heat and add the mayocoba beans, crushed red pepper flakes, cumin, bay leaf, vegetable broth, salt and pepper. Allow the beans to simmer for 10 minutes. Remove the bay leaf, and use a bean smasher or hand-held emulsifier to smash the beans into a rough and slightly runny paste. Taste for seasoning, and add more as needed.

To make the sopes, preheat a comal or griddle over medium heat. Divide the masa into ¼-cup (65-g) balls. You should have 12 balls. Use your hands to press the masa into thick 4-inch (10-cm) round disks, using your fingers to gently press any cracked edges. These will be thicker than tortillas and will take slightly longer to cook. Place each sope on the comal to cook for about 2 minutes. When the first side sears and the edges start to slightly dry, flip it over to the second side and cook for 2 more minutes. Flip the sope again and remove to a plate to slightly cool. Once each sope is cool enough to handle, use your fingers to pinch the edges, forming a rim around the edge of each sope. Put them back on the comal to heat through.

To make the avocado salsa, add the tomatillos, jalapeño, lemon juice, cumin, avocado, cilantro and salt to a blender. Blend until smooth. Taste for lemon juice and salt, and add more as needed.

To serve, add a layer of mayocoba beans to the bottom of each sope. It should be enough to fill the rim of the sope. Add the walnut meat over the beans, and top it with the salsa. Garnish with Queso Añejo and cilantro.

MOLE VERDE CON CHAMPIÑONES

(Mushrooms in Green Mole)

There are several varieties of mole throughout Mexico from mole Colorado to mole verde and pipián. Each one has a distinct color, flavor and aroma that makes it so incredibly special. Many dark and rich mole sauces layer flavors from dried and toasted nuts, seeds and chiles. Mole Verde is distinctly different since it is made with many fresh ingredients like cilantro, romaine lettuce, epazote, serranos and tomatillos. The cilantro, fresh chiles and tomatillos give this mole a bright slightly acidic flavor, while the toasted seeds and epazote ground all the flavors. Many of the dark mole recipes can take days and many hours to prepare, but this recipe will take a few hours to prepare.

This mole recipe is light and tangy and can be paired with anything from seared mushrooms—like we're doing here—to rice and roasted veggies.

YIELD: 4 SERVINGS

For the Mole

1 cup (140 g) brown sesame seeds

½ cup (65 g) pepitas

3 dried allspice berries

8 tomatillos, peeled and washed

3 serrano chiles, destemmed (deveined if too spicy)

4 cloves garlic

½ white onion

2 cups (480 ml) vegetable broth, divided, plus more as needed

¼ cup (60 ml) cooking oil, plus more as needed

6–8 medium romaine lettuce leaves

6 epazote leaves

1 bunch cilantro

Salt and pepper, to taste

For the Mushrooms

3 tbsp (45 ml) cooking oil, plus more for cooking as needed

1½ lbs (680 g) mushroom varieties of choice

¼ tsp ground cumin

Salt and pepper, to taste

For Serving

Cilantro, to garnish

Sesame seeds, to garnish

Pepitas, to garnish

Tortillas Hechas a Mano (page 98), for serving

To make the mole, add the sesame seeds to a dry skillet and heat over medium heat. Stir constantly for 4 to 5 minutes, or until the seeds become fragrant and a deep golden color. Place them on a plate to cool. Add the pepitas to the same pan to toast. Stir them constantly for 4 to 5 minutes, or until they become fragrant and start to puff and pop. Place them on a plate to cool. Lightly toast the allspice berries in the same skillet for 2 to 3 minutes until they become fragrant. Remove from the skillet and set aside. Add the tomatillos, serrano chiles, garlic and onion to the same skillet to char on all sides for about 10 to 15 minutes, until their colors deepen and they cook through.

(Continued)

Add the toasted seeds and allspice to a blender with 1 cup (240 ml) of the vegetable broth, and blend until smooth. Add more broth as needed to make a paste.

Add the oil to the bottom of a medium pot over medium heat, and add the seed paste. Stir constantly to avoid sticking, adding more oil as needed until the paste becomes a deep golden color.

Add the charred tomatillos, serranos, garlic, onion, romaine leaves, epazote leaves and cilantro to a blender. Blend until smooth. You may need to blend these ingredients in batches if your blender cup is small. Add the mixture to the pan with the seed paste over medium heat and stir until the ingredients are fully incorporated. Season with salt and pepper and continue cooking over medium heat for 10 minutes, or until the sauce thickens. Stir constantly to avoid sticking. Add the remaining 1 cup (240 ml) of broth and cook for 10 minutes. Taste for salt and add more as needed.

When making the mushrooms, I like to use a few varieties for different flavors and textures. Add the oil to the bottom of a sauté pan and preheat over medium heat. When the oil is hot, add the mushrooms to sear on all sides. Season the mushrooms with cumin, salt and pepper. Different mushrooms sizes will have different cooking times, so constantly check the level of doneness of each type of mushroom.

Add the mole to a serving plate and top with the mushrooms. Garnish with cilantro, sesame seeds and pepitas. Serve with Tortillas Hechas a Mano.

TACOS DE JAMAICA
(Hibiscus Flower Tacos)

Flor de jamaica or hibiscus flowers are often used to make a traditional jamaica *agua fresca* sweetened with cane sugar, and sometimes paired with fresh herbs like *yerba buena*. Jamaica is an acidic flower that grows in hot and tropical areas and is loaded with antioxidants, which supports kidney health and aids in reducing blood pressure. It's rarely used for any recipes in Mexico aside from agua fresca.

For this recipe, we'll be cooking down the flor de jamaica to make a savory taco filling. We'll need to boil the jamaica twice to get rid of the acidity, but you can save some of the boiling water from the first round to make jamaica agua fresca.

YIELD: 4–6 SERVINGS

3 cups (120 g) dried jamaica flowers

8 cups (2 L) water, divided

1 large globe tomato, quartered

3 cloves garlic, peeled

⅓ cup (80 ml) cooking oil, divided, plus more for cooking as needed

¼ red onion, thinly sliced

Salt, to taste

1 tsp ground cumin

1 tsp dried oregano

1 serrano chile, minced and deseeded (if too spicy)

1–2 tbsp (15–30 ml) chipotle adobo sauce

2 tbsp (30 ml) orange juice

Tortillas Hechas a Mano (page 98), for serving

Avocado slices, to garnish

Crema de Anacardo (page 117), to garnish

Wash the jamaica flowers in a strainer. Add 4 cups (960 ml) of the water and the flowers to a medium pot. Bring to a boil and cook for about 15 minutes. Strain the water from the pot. (You can keep this water to make a jamaica agua fresca.) Rinse the jamaica flowers in a strainer again. Add the remaining water and the jamaica flowers to the same pot and bring to a boil for another 15 minutes. Strain the jamaica leaves and set aside.

While the jamaica leaves are boiling, you can prepare the other ingredients. Put the tomato in a blender with the garlic. Blend until smooth and set aside.

Coat a sauté pan with 2 tablespoons (30 ml) of the oil and preheat over medium-low heat. Add the onion and salt and sauté for about 5 minutes, or until slightly soft and translucent. Add the cumin and oregano and sauté for 1 minute. Add the remaining oil, strained jamaica leaves and more salt. Sauté until the ingredients are well incorporated. Add the tomato mixture from the blender and the serrano chile, chipotle adobo sauce and orange juice and sauté for 15 to 20 minutes, or until the liquid slightly evaporates and the jamaica leaves soften and the flavors meld together. Add additional oil as needed. Serve on a freshly made Tortillas Hechas a Mano with avocado slices and Crema de Anacardo over the top.

PLATOS ADICIONALES

Side Dishes

Have you ever made a side dish and eaten it as an entrée? Maybe it was a long day, or a long week, and you've mustered up the energy to reheat some leftovers or put together something that's easy and filling. For many of those days, a simple bowl of *frijoles de la olla* (beans in a pot) with rice and a little bit of salsa has been just that. These are the ultimate comfort staples that typically accompany main dishes. But these recipes stand alone in their own right with bold flavors and heartiness. I think everything on the plate should be flavorful and thoughtful on its own.

In this chapter, we'll be cooking side staples like two versions of brown rice, smashed beans, fresh Tortillas Hechas a Mano (page 98) and Pan de Elote (page 101). They are all simple recipes that pack a punch of flavor and will complete a main dish. You can always double a batch to have a side already cooked, prepared and sitting in the fridge so it's ready to use throughout the week to make dinner on weeknights a little faster to prepare.

ARROZ CON CILANTRO

(Cilantro Brown Rice)

Cilantro is a magical herb that thankfully found its way to Mexican cuisine all the way from southern Europe and North Africa. It has forever shaped the cuisine as a garnish and ingredient that offers a distinct fresh flavor. The flavor transforms when it's cooked in dishes like cooked stews and soups or grilled to offer a deeper savory flavor profile.

In this recipe, we'll be making a simple cilantro stock to cook our rice that will not only permeate the rice with a rich flavor but will also transform it to a beautiful green. Sometimes I even serve this dish at room temperature as more of a salad with greens and minced cilantro mixed in for added texture. I really love this rice dish served with Pipián Rojo con Yaca (page 80) over the top.

YIELD: 4-6 SERVINGS

½ bunch cilantro

2¾ cups (660 ml) vegetable broth

¼ cup (60 ml) cooking oil

1¾ cups (350 g) uncooked short-grain brown rice, rinsed and strained

1½ tsp (2 g) crushed red pepper flakes

½ tsp ground cumin

2 bay leaves

Salt and pepper, to taste

Place the cilantro and vegetable broth in a blender. (Reserve a few cilantro sprigs to garnish.) Blend until smooth and set aside.

Preheat a medium pot over medium heat and add the oil. Add the rice and toast for 5 to 10 minutes, or until lightly toasted, golden brown and fragrant, stirring frequently so it cooks evenly. Add the cilantro broth, crushed red pepper flakes, cumin, bay leaves, salt and pepper. Stir once to make sure the seasoning is mixed in and all the rice is submerged. Place the lid slightly ajar over the pot, and cook over medium-low heat for 40 to 45 minutes, or until tender. Discard the bay leaves and serve the rice in a large dish and garnish with a few sprigs of cilantro.

ARROZ MEXICANO

(Mexican Brown Rice)

Mexican rice is commonly called Spanish rice because the Spaniards brought rice traveling from Asia to Mexico. These rice variations, though slightly similar, are completely different, with notes of different spices. Mexican rice uses native tomatoes for the vibrant, slightly orange/red hue with spices like cumin and chiles, while Spanish rice uses saffron for a yellow/red hue and distinctly different flavor.

For this recipe variation, we're using brown rice instead of white rice for added texture and more whole-grain goodness. You can use canned tomato sauce or make your own by blending fresh ripe tomatoes. This rice pairs well with Fajitas de Champiñones (page 65).

YIELD: 4–6 SERVINGS

¼ cup (60 ml) cooking oil

1¾ cups (350 g) uncooked short-grain brown rice, rinsed and strained

¾ cup (180 ml) tomato sauce

2¾ cups (660 ml) vegetable broth

1½ tsp (2 g) crushed red pepper flakes

½ tsp ground cumin

2 bay leaves

Salt and pepper, to taste

Cilantro sprigs, to garnish

Preheat a medium pot over medium heat, and add the oil. Toast the rice for 5 to 10 minutes, or until lightly toasted, golden brown and fragrant, stirring frequently so it cooks evenly. Add the tomato sauce, vegetable broth, crushed red pepper flakes, cumin, bay leaves, salt and pepper. Stir once to make sure the seasoning is mixed in and all the rice is submerged. Place the lid slightly ajar over the pot, and cook over medium-low heat for 40 to 45 minutes, or until tender. Serve the rice in a large dish and garnish with a few sprigs of cilantro.

FRIJOLES NEGROS

(Black Beans)

Frijoles negros are also known as turtle beans, and they have been a sustaining staple throughout Central and South America. They are seen mostly in the southern regions of Mexico, carrying more fiber and antioxidants than the beloved pinto bean. I love to cook a pot of beans for the week that can be used in salads, as a side dish or refried. In this recipe, we'll be smashing our cooked beans with spices and vegetable broth.

YIELD: 4–6 SERVINGS

¼ cup (60 ml) cooking oil

3 cups (516 g) cooked black beans, strained

½ tsp crushed red pepper flakes

½ tsp ground cumin

1 bay leaf

1 cup (240 ml) vegetable broth

Salt and pepper, to taste

Queso Añejo (page 29), to garnish

Cilantro sprigs, to garnish

Preheat a medium pot over medium heat, and coat the bottom of the pot with the oil. Add the black beans, crushed red pepper flakes, cumin, bay leaf, vegetable broth, salt and pepper. Allow the beans to simmer for 10 to 15 minutes. Remove the bay leaf, and use a bean smasher or hand-held emulsifier to smash the beans into a rough and slightly runny paste. Taste for seasoning, and add more as needed. Serve in a large dish and garnish with Queso Añejo and a few sprigs of cilantro.

CHEF'S NOTE: If you are cooking dried beans, it's best to soak them overnight. Strain the water and cover with 2 inches (5 cm) of fresh water with bay leaves and salt. Cook the beans until they are tender and creamy, adding more water as needed to keep them submerged.

TORTILLAS HECHAS A MANO
(Handmade Tortillas)

Corn tortillas are the foundation of Mexican cuisine and are used as a side to pile on main ingredients, cheeses and salsas to make tacos. They are also cut into pieces and fried to make tortilla chips for dishes like chilaquiles, toasted or fried to hold up dishes like ceviche or tinga and are even used as a sauce binder. Tortillas are a versatile cornerstone that will most likely show up across kitchen tables in Mexican households in one way or another.

Fresh *tortillas hechas a mano* can be made from nixtamalized organic corn or organic masa harina. You can also check if your local tortilleria has an organic GMO-free option. Corn can typically be purchased in either white, yellow or blue varieties. If you're picking up masa harina or corn flour to make your own masa, be sure it has gone through the nixtamal process of being cooked and soaked in calcium hydroxide or cal. This process creates an alkaline solution that releases the hull from the corn kernel and makes for a more nutritious ingredient.

For this recipe, we'll be using store-bought masa harina to make our masa. I prefer brands such as Bob's Red Mill, Masienda and Gold Mine, which can be purchased online or at your local health food store.

YIELD: 6-8 SERVINGS

2 cups (230 g) organic masa harina

2–3 cups (480–720 ml) hot water

¼ cup (60 ml) cooking oil, divided

Salt, to taste

Add the masa harina to a medium bowl. Pour in 2 cups (480 ml) of hot water, and use your hands or a spoon to mix the masa. Slowly add more water as needed. Once the masa starts to form into a dough, continue to use your hands to *amasar*, or knead, the masa to bring it all together. The masa should be a Play-Doh–like consistency that sticks together and doesn't stick to the bowl or your hands. Add 1 tablespoon (15 ml) of the oil and salt to taste, and continue to knead the masa, adding more oil as needed, up to ¼ cup (60 ml).

Preheat a comal or skillet to medium-high heat.

Roll the masa into small walnut-sized balls. Use a *prensa* or tortilla press lined with plastic or wax paper to press the tortillas evenly until the *masa* becomes a tortilla about 4 to 5 inches (10 to 13 cm) in diameter. You can also use your hands to pat the tortilla down between the plastic or wax paper if you don't have a tortilla press, or add your masa ball to a cutting board lined with plastic or wax paper that's long enough to fold over the top of the ball (giving space for the masa to spread out). Add another cutting board over the top or a clear glass oven dish, and use your hands to evenly press down until the masa is flattened evenly.

Add the first tortilla to the preheated comal. Let it cook for about 20 seconds, or until the first side begins to sear and the outer layer of the tortilla seals. The tortilla should release from the comal or griddle. Flip the tortilla to cook on the second side for 20 seconds. Flip it back to the original side, and the tortilla may start to puff up after another 20 seconds. Repeat for all the tortillas. Place the cooked tortillas in a tortilla holder lined with a cloth towel to keep them warm. They will continue to steam and cook in the basket.

PAN DE ELOTE

(Gluten-Free Cornbread)

Cornbread is a side dish that has been made by native communities for many years. It was a dense bread that later evolved to a fluffy cake with new ingredients like chicken eggs and buttermilk. In Mexico, *pan de elote* is creamy and almost the consistency of bread pudding. It is mostly made of eggs and condensed milk with flour and corn to bind it all together.

For this recipe, we'll be exploring the intersection of these versions of corn-based bread for a moist bread that also holds its shape. This version is moist and dense—the in-between of a creamy bread pudding and moist cornbread.

YIELD: 6-8 SERVINGS

1 cup (115 g) corn flour (or cornmeal blended smooth)

6 tbsp (66 g) oat flour (or whole oats blended smooth)

½ cup (90 g) raw sugar

2 tbsp (20 g) baking powder

½ tsp baking soda

Pinch of salt

4 tbsp (19 g) egg replacer, such as Follow Your Heart VeganEgg

1 cup (240 ml) ice cold water

¾ cup (180 ml) unsweetened almond milk

½ cup (120 ml), plus 1 tbsp (15 ml) melted vegan butter

¼ cup (60 ml) applesauce

¼ cup (60 ml) cooking oil

4 ears corn

Preheat an oven to 350°F (180°C).

Add to a medium bowl the corn flour, oat flour, sugar, baking powder, baking soda and a pinch of salt. Use a whisk to combine.

In a separate bowl, add the egg replacer and water. Whisk until smooth. Add the almond milk, ½ cup (120 ml) of the melted butter, applesauce and oil to the bowl and whisk to combine. Cut the corn kernels off the cob and add to the bowl.

Form a well in the center of the dry ingredients and slowly pour in the wet ingredients, whisking as you pour to fully incorporate the ingredients.

Use the 1 tablespoon (15 ml) of melted vegan butter to grease a 9-inch (23-cm) cast-iron skillet or baking pan. Add the batter to the skillet and place in the oven. Let the bread bake for 45 to 50 minutes, or until it's golden brown and a toothpick or fork comes out clean after piercing the center of the bread. Take the bread out of the oven and allow it to set and cool for 20 to 30 minutes before serving.

SALSAS

There are more than 150 different varieties of chiles from fresh, dried, small and large, with more varietal possibilities as the plants cross-pollinate. Indigenous communities have harvested and used chiles in their cuisine for generations. Chiles are native to the New World and have changed cuisine around the world forever through the spice trade. They serve as a flavor enhancer and are also used as medicines with antioxidant and anti-inflammatory properties that aid digestion, improve immunity and reduce heart disease.

These different chile varieties can make hundreds of salsa combinations that can be used as marinades or to top a dish. Salsas offer an acidic, salty and spicy note that can completely transform and brighten any dish. Some chiles like serranos or habañeros offer a much spicier piquancy, so a little goes a long way. Typically, the smaller the chile pepper, the higher the capsaicin or fiery kick.

Salsas have been the foundation of Mexican cooking with salsa ingredients ground down into a sauce in a *molcajete* made of volcanic stone. You're welcome to use a molcajete to make these salsas, but today, blenders are used to make the process easier.

GUACAMOLE CON SEMILLAS

(Guacamole with Seeds)

The Nahuatl word for avocado is *āhuacatl*, which is pronounced *aguacate* in Spanish. The Spanish word *mole* means sauce and stems from the Nahuatl word *mōlli*. Guacamole is the merger of these two words, which means avocado sauce. It is typically prepared with tomato, onion and chile, with many variations throughout different regions of Mexico.

Guacamole is a simple recipe packed with so much flavor. It can be eaten with tortilla chips or used to top dishes like tacos. This recipe is filled with seeds that give it a crunchy texture and a multitude of health benefits.

YIELD: 4–6 SERVINGS

1 serrano chile

2 medium Hass avocados, mashed

¼ cup (60 ml) lemon juice

1 Roma tomato, diced

½ bunch cilantro, minced

1 tbsp (9 g) toasted pepitas

1 tbsp (8 g) toasted sunflower seeds

1 tbsp (9 g) toasted white or golden sesame seeds

1 tbsp (10 g) hemp seeds

1 tbsp (12 g) white chia seeds

1 tbsp (10 g) flax seeds

Salt and pepper, to taste

1 (16-oz [454-g]) bag tortilla chips

Turn a burner to high heat. Using heatproof tongs, hold the serrano chile pepper over the open flame and turn evenly for 3 to 5 minutes until the skin is charred and blistered and the chile is tender. Once the serrano has come to room temperature, destem, dice into ⅛-inch (3-mm) pieces and set aside.

Put the avocados and lemon juice in a medium bowl and mash with a bean masher until it is a chunky consistency. Fold in the tomato, cilantro, serrano, pepitas, sunflower seeds, sesame seeds, hemp seeds, chia seeds, flax seeds, salt and pepper. If the mixture is too thick, you can loosen the guacamole with more lemon juice or a little water. Taste for seasoning and add more as needed. Serve in a large dish and garnish with more seeds. Serve with tortilla chips.

CHILE DE ÁRBOL Y TOMATILLO

(Arbol Chiles with Tomatillo)

My abuelita would make this salsa to finish her gorditas, or just to have as an option on the table for many of our family meals. The few charred *chile de árbol* made the whole kitchen fragrant with spicy clouds of smoke released from the heat. We'd all walk into the kitchen and immediately start coughing, which then made us all laugh because she got us. It was always a challenge to see who could withstand the fiery, spicy air without flinching. She always won.

This recipe is incredibly easy to make and is tangy from the tomatillos with lots of heat from the chiles de árbol. We grew up making this salsa recipe in a molcajete, and I recommend you try this grinding method to release more of the oils from the chiles. If you don't have a molcajete readily available, you can use a blender.

YIELD: 4-6 SERVINGS

2–3 dried chiles de árbol

½ cup (120 ml) water

Salt, to taste

6 large tomatillos, husks removed and washed

Add the chiles de árbol to a dry skillet. Turn the heat to medium, and flip the chiles around for 1 minute until they start to slightly blacken and release a spicy smoke. Add the blackened chiles to the water to rehydrate for about 10 minutes.

Once the chiles are tender, place them in the molcajete with salt and a splash of the water used to rehydrate the chiles. Break down the chiles until they become a paste, adding more of the water used to rehydrate the chiles as needed.

Add the tomatillos to a hot skillet over medium heat. Once the tomatillos are charred and blackened on one side, use tongs to flip them over to char on the other side until fully blackened and blistered on all sides, about 10 to 15 minutes total. Add the charred and tender tomatillos to the molcajete one-by-one with the chile de árbol paste. Grind them each down until you reach a slightly chunky salsa consistency. Add salt to taste and serve in the molcajete.

SALSA ROJA DE TOMATE

(Red Tomato Salsa)

Tomatoes are an ingredient native to the Americas that were introduced to Europeans during colonization and changed food culture around the world. It's a versatile ingredient that can be used in so many ways that can take dishes in completely different directions depending on the level of sweetness or acidity.

For this recipe, the tomatoes are the base for a tangy and mildly spicy salsa that can be used to top dishes like tacos or can simply be served with chips. This is a recipe you can make and store in the fridge, so it's ready to eat on busy evenings after work.

YIELD: 4–6 SERVINGS

3 medium globe tomatoes

1–2 serrano chiles, destemmed (deveined if too spicy)

⅛ tsp ground cumin

Salt, to taste

2 tbsp (30 ml) cooking oil

¼ bunch cilantro, minced

1–2 tbsp (15–30 ml) lemon juice

Turn on a burner to medium-high heat. Using heatproof tongs, cook the tomatoes and serrano chiles over the open flame for about 8 to 10 minutes until they are charred and tender. Add the tomatoes and serranos to a blender with the cumin and salt, and blend until smooth.

Coat the bottom of a pan with the oil and preheat over medium heat. When the oil is hot, carefully pour in the tomato mixture. Reduce the heat to low, and allow the salsa to simmer for 5 to 10 minutes, or until it deepens in color and slightly reduces. Turn off the heat, and add the cilantro and lemon juice to brighten the salsa.

SALSA DE TOMATILLO

(Tomatillo Salsa)

Tomatillos are a part of the nightshade family and commonly confused for green tomatoes since their name translates to "little tomato." It's papery, inedible husk makes it a relative of the gooseberry. The flavor of tomatillos is distinctly tart and it can be eaten raw or cooked, which mellows its acidity.

I love using this tomatillo salsa recipe to make chilaquiles, which is a common Mexican breakfast dish. It's just a few extra steps towards the perfect brunch dish. It's another great salsa to have on hand in the fridge for the week. A good zero-waste trick is to make a batch or two of this salsa and add it to jars while it's hot to have a delicious homemade salsa waiting in your pantry whenever you need it.

YIELD: 4–6 SERVINGS

8 large tomatillos, husks removed and washed

1–2 jalapeños, destemmed (deveined if too spicy)

⅛ tsp ground cumin

Salt, to taste

2 tbsp (30 ml) cooking oil

¼ bunch cilantro, minced

1–2 tbsp (15–30 ml) lemon juice

Turn on a burner to medium-high heat. Using heatproof tongs, cook the tomatillos and jalapeños over the flame for about 5 to 8 minutes until they are charred and tender. Add the tomatillos and jalapeños to a blender with the cumin and salt, and blend until smooth.

Coat the bottom of a pan with the oil, and preheat over medium heat. When the oil is hot, carefully pour in the tomatillo mixture. Reduce the heat to low, and allow the salsa to simmer for 5 to 10 minutes, or until it deepens in color and slightly reduces. Turn off the heat, and add the cilantro and lemon juice to brighten the salsa.

CHEF'S NOTE: Once you complete this recipe, you can make chilaquiles by adding some vegetable broth to the salsa in the pan to loosen it and allow it to come to a simmer. Add tortilla chips, and gently toss them in the salsa until they are fully coated. Top your chilaquiles with Crema de Anacardo (page 117) and Queso Fresco (page 26) to balance out the acidity of the tomatillos.

SALSA DE TAMARINDO

(Tamarind Salsa)

Tamarind is a fruit in a pod that contains a sticky and sour pulp that traveled to Mexico from its native land of Africa. It is mostly used in Mexico as an agua fresca ingredient, candied or in a dessert. It is typically not seen in savory dishes, but it is sometimes used in meat marinades.

In this salsa recipe, the tamarind pulp will be paired with mild guajillo and ancho chiles to create a slightly sweet-and-tangy salsa that can be added to dishes or eaten with tortilla chips. The tamarind pulp has many seeds that can be a bit tricky to remove. A tip is to soak the pulp in water so it becomes softer and easier to deseed. You can also find small jars of tamarind paste that is already completely seedless.

YIELD: 4-6 SERVINGS

1 tbsp (15 ml) cooking oil

3 dried ancho chiles, washed, destemmed and deseeded

3 dried guajillo chiles, washed, destemmed and deseeded

1 cup (240 ml) water

3 tbsp (45 ml) seedless tamarind paste

Salt, to taste

Preheat a medium saucepan over medium heat. Add the oil, the ancho chiles and the guajillo chiles and panfry for 1 minute until the chiles are slightly blackened on both sides. Place the blackened chiles into a mixing bowl with the water for 10 minutes to rehydrate. Place another mixing bowl over the chiles to keep them submerged in the water.

Put the rehydrated chiles in a blender with the tamarind paste, ¾ cup (180 ml) of the water from the mixing bowl used to rehydrate the chiles and salt. Blend until smooth, and add more water from the chile-soaking water if necessary to create a sauce consistency.

SALSA DE CHIPOTLE
(Chipotle Salsa)

Chipotle chiles start out as jalapeños that are ripe and smoked. They have a distinct smoky flavor that slightly changes depending on the variety of chile. You can find chipotle morita, meco, ground powder and in adobo sauce at most Mexican grocery stores or online.

For this recipe, we are using chipotle in adobo for a tangy, smoky and slightly sweet salsa with a kick of heat. Chipotle in adobo can be purchased canned, and the chipotle chiles are in a wet adobo paste. I like to blend my chipotles into the adobo paste and store it in the fridge as paste. This way I use a spoonful of paste as a chile.

YIELD: 4-6 SERVINGS

3 medium globe tomatoes

2–3 chipotle chiles in adobo sauce

1 tbsp (15 ml) lemon juice

⅛ tsp cumin

Salt, to taste

2 tbsp (30 ml) cooking oil

¼ bunch cilantro, minced

Turn a burner on to high heat. Using heatproof tongs, cook the tomatoes over the open flame for 10 minutes until they are charred and tender. Turn them to cook on all sides. Add the charred tomatoes, chipotle chiles, lemon juice, cumin and salt to a blender. Blend until smooth, and set aside.

Coat the bottom of a sauté pan with the oil and preheat over medium heat. When the oil is hot, add the chipotle salsa to the pan (pouring away from you to avoid spattering). Cook the salsa for 5 to 10 minutes, or until it starts to turn a deep red color and thickens and bubbles. Allow the mixture to cool and mix in the cilantro.

CREMA DE ANACARDO
(Cashew Cream)

We go through jars and jars of Cashew Crema regularly through our Todo Verde catering events and weekly pop-ups. It's something our customers love because it's tangy and gives a pop of flavor to any dish you choose to top with crema. This would be a time when the sarcastic phrase commonly used in Mexico City, "*No le eches tanta crema a tus tacos*" (Don't put so much cream on your tacos), does not apply.

Cashews are a great base because they provide a creamy texture, and their flavor is so mild that it can easily be disguised with a few more ingredients. The probiotic capsules can be purchased in the refrigerated section of your local health food store and allow the cream to ferment to give it the true flavor of a Mexican crema.

YIELD: 4-6 SERVINGS

¾ cup (110 g) raw cashew pieces, soaked and rinsed (see Note)

½ cup (120 ml) water

2 acidophilus probiotic capsules

1–2 tbsp (15–30 ml) lemon juice

1 tsp nutritional yeast

Salt, to taste (start with 1 tsp, it should be slightly salty)

Add the soaked and drained cashew pieces to a blender with the water and blend until completely smooth. Scrape down the sides of the blender with a spatula to get any bits that didn't blend, and add more water if necessary to create a thick and creamy consistency. Once smooth, add the probiotic powder from the capsules, and discard the casings. Pulse with the blender to incorporate the probiotic powder. Use a spatula to scrape the cream out of the blender and into a glass bowl. Cover the bowl with a cheesecloth, a mesh bag or plastic wrap with holes poked in. Allow the mixture to sit at room temperature and ferment for 15 to 18 hours, or until it's tangy and cheesy.

Add the lemon juice, nutritional yeast and salt and mix until fully incorporated. Taste for salt and lemon juice and add more as needed.

CHEF'S NOTE: Cashews should be soaked for 2 hours if you don't have a high-power blender, and at least 30 minutes in warm water if you do have one.

DULCE

Sweets

This chapter honors what I think desserts should be: a balanced and sweet end to a satisfying meal. The desserts in this chapter give you just enough craveable sweetness to tell your friends about it. There's nothing like a delicious *postre* to end a celebratory savory meal.

Sweets are something to enjoy in moderation without all the guilt. The real key is to be mindful of everything you eat regularly, and include food that nourishes our bodies every day. Our ancestors ate desserts sweetened with raw cane sugar, and they didn't deal with some of the preventable diseases we see in our communities today. So I don't blame the sweets anymore. Instead, I work on improving my lifestyle choices.

In this chapter, we'll be making dishes ranging from sweet and fluffy Tamales de Fresa con Rosa (page 121), two different ice cream flavors, Pudín de Cacao (page 126), Capirotada de Xocolate (page 134) and more. We'll use unrefined raw cane sugar and pure maple syrup to sweeten these treats. My favorite recipe in this chapter is Arroz con Leche Negro (page 125) since this was a dish my mom prepared for special occasions like birthdays or good report cards.

TAMALES DE FRESA CON ROSA

(Strawberry-Rose Tamales)

Todo Verde is known for its strawberry-rose recipes—with our Amorcito agua fresca made from strawberry, rose, chia and maple syrup being one of our most requested items. We've used this flavor combination to make hot milk tea, cheesecake and more. So it only seemed right to test it as a sweet tamale recipe, and it's just as good as we imagined.

For this recipe, we'll be working with yellow corn masa harina that will be stained pink from the fresh strawberries. We'll make a creamy sweet masa that will be steamed to make fluffy and aromatic rose and strawberry corn cakes.

YIELD: 4 SERVINGS

24 dried corn husks

1 cup (240 ml) unsweetened almond milk

2 cups (288 g) strawberries

3 cups (345 g) organic masa harina

1 cup (240 ml) hot water

½–¾ cup (120–180 ml) melted refined coconut oil (with no scent or coconut flavor)

4 tbsp (56 g) vegan butter, softened

¾ cup (135 g) raw sugar

1 tbsp (10 g) baking powder

1 tbsp (15 ml) rose water

Pinch of salt

Dried rose petals, to garnish

Immerse the corn husks in a large bowl or bucket of warm water. Use a plate or bowl to hold them below water level, if needed. The corn husks should soak for at least 30 minutes, but 3 hours to overnight is best.

Put the almond milk and strawberries in a blender, and blend until smooth. Set aside.

Pour the masa harina in a large bowl and slowly add in the hot water. Mix with a silicone spatula to incorporate the water. Add the coconut oil (starting with ½ cup [120 ml]), vegan butter, strawberry mixture, sugar, baking powder, rose water and salt. Mix until all ingredients are fully incorporated and create a loose dough. Let the masa rest at room temperature for 30 minutes. If the masa looks dry, you can add the remaining coconut oil.

Remove the soaked corn husks from the water once they are pliable and soft to the touch and pat them dry with a towel. Smear 4 to 5 spoonfuls of masa on the edge of the wider end of the corn husk. You can use one large corn husk per tamale or 2 smaller husks stacked slightly side by side to create a larger surface. To fold the tamale, start with folding the right side of the husk over the tamale, then fold the left side of the husk over the right. Fold the narrow point of the husk towards the folded husks. If you have leftover husks, you can tear them into lengthwise strips used to tie each tamale.

Add 1 to 2 inches (2.5 to 5 cm) of water to a large pot. Add a pot steamer to the bottom of the pot, so the tamales do not touch the water. Bring to a simmer over medium-high heat. Add the tamales to the steamer with the open ends facing up. Start by standing them around the edge of the pot, then add the remaining tamales to the center of the pot. Cover the pot, and steam the tamales for 45 minutes, or until the masa is cooked through and fluffy. When serving, open the corn husk to reveal the tamale, and garnish with crumbled dried rose petals.

FLAN DE COCO
(Coconut Flan)

Flan is one of the most popular desserts in Mexican food culture. It's an egg, cream and sugar recipe that has traveled continents and time and still remains relatively intact in terms of flavor and texture. It's served at most special occasions and is on the menu throughout most of LA's Mexican restaurants. There are now more flavor variations like citrus-flavored flan, *rompope* flan or even chocoflan.

For this flan recipe, we're making a coconut-flavored base and using egg replacer to give that rich egg flavor that makes a flan, *flan*. This recipe has four main steps that pull it all together, but it's definitely worth the effort.

YIELD: 3-4 SERVINGS

For the Syrup

6 tbsp (85 g) raw sugar

¼ cup (60 ml) water

For the Flan

1½ cups (360 ml) canned unsweetened coconut milk

⅓ cup (80 ml) unsweetened coconut cream

2 tbsp (4 g) flaky agar or 1½ tsp (4 g) fine agar

2 tbsp (10 g) egg replacer, such as Follow Your Heart VeganEgg

½ cup (120 ml) ice-cold water

2 tbsp (32 g) strained and squeezed extra-firm tofu

¼ cup (45 g) raw sugar

1 tbsp (15 ml) vanilla

Pinch of turmeric, for color

Pinch of salt

For Serving

¼ cup (8 g) marigold petals, or another edible flower

To make the syrup, melt down the sugar and water in a small pot until the crystals dissolve. Add the syrup to the bottom of a 6-inch (15-cm) mold or 3 small (2-inch [5-cm]) molds for individual servings.

To make the flan, add the coconut milk, coconut cream and agar flakes to a saucepan. Let it sit for 10 minutes, and then bring to a simmer while whisking constantly. Reduce the heat to low, whisking until all the agar flakes completely dissolves. Take the pan off of the heat and set aside.

Combine the egg replacer with the ice-cold water in a medium bowl. Slowly whisk until the mixture is completely smooth. Set aside.

Place the tofu, sugar, vanilla, turmeric and salt in blender and blend until completely smooth. Add the blended tofu mixture to the hot coconut and agar mixture and whisk to combine. Slowly pour the coconut-tofu mixture into the egg replacer bowl while whisking. Whisk until completely smooth. Pour the mixture into the flan mold(s) over the syrup. Cover the dish with plastic wrap, and refrigerate for at least 2 hours.

To remove from the baking dish, dip into hot water for 15 seconds, then flip onto a platter. Serve the flan on a platter and top with edible flower petals in a ring around the edge of the flan.

CHEF'S NOTE: If you can't find edible flowers, you can use toasted coconut shreds as a garnish.

The egg replacer should be a product that can make a plant-based scrambled egg, and not a binder for baking such as flax seeds or chia.

ARROZ CON LECHE NEGRO
(Black Rice Pudding)

Birthdays and good grades were equally important reasons to celebrate in our home. If I came home with a report card showing all As, my parents would ask what I wanted to eat for dinner that night. Sometimes we would go out to a Sizzler just blocks away from our house in South Gate for a *fancy* meal, and other times I would ask for dishes like my mom's signature *arroz con leche*. It was creamy, cinnamon-spiced and filled with black raisins for added texture and sweetness.

When I first started making my homemade version, my mom thought I was crazy for using black rice instead of the traditional white rice. Black rice adds nutrients, creates more texture . . . and I love the color. I added golden raisins instead of black raisins to create a color contrast against the black rice. When she finally tried it, she was shocked that all the familiar flavors were still there. The black rice can be slightly chewier than white rice, so it's important to soak the rice to create a similar texture.

YIELD: 4–6 SERVINGS

2 cups (345 g) uncooked rinsed black rice

2 cups (480 ml) water

1 whole Mexican cinnamon stick

½ cup (90 g) raw sugar

½ cup (120 ml) pure maple syrup

2½ cups (600 ml) unsweetened almond milk

¼ cup (42 g) golden raisins, plus more to garnish

¼ cup (60 ml) vanilla

Pinch of salt

1 tsp ground Mexican cinnamon, to garnish

Rinse and soak the black rice in water for at least 3 hours. Set aside.

Pour in the water and add the cinnamon stick to a medium pot over medium heat and bring to a boil. Once the cinnamon has diffused in the water, add the rice, sugar, maple syrup and almond milk. Allow the mixture to come to a boil, then lower the heat to medium-low and allow to simmer for 45 to 55 minutes, or until the rice is tender and half of the liquid has been absorbed. Remove the cinnamon stick, and add the raisins, vanilla and salt.

Serve with more raisins and a sprinkle of ground cinnamon for garnish.

CHEF'S NOTE: If you don't have a Mexican cinnamon stick, replace it in this recipe with 1 tablespoon (8 g) of ground Mexican cinnamon.

PUDÍN DE CACAO

(Cacao Pudding)

Growing up, eating chocolate pudding cups was a highlight. We didn't always have them stocked up in our fridge, so when we did, I always made a point to try to eat them often before my brother got through all of them. There was something so rich and decadent about that creamy chocolate pudding packed in little plastic cups. The best part was licking the pudding stuck to the aluminum lid before you dug into the cup with your spoon.

For this recipe, we'll be making a creamy rich base from avocados! The raw cacao and cinnamon, cayenne and sea salt will give it a Mexican-spiced flavor. We'll finish this pudding cup off with some bright red strawberry wedges and crushed pistachio for texture.

YIELD: 4 SERVINGS

2 medium Hass avocados

¼ cup (28 g) cacao powder

1½ tsp (4 g) ground Mexican cinnamon, plus extra if needed

Pinch of cayenne

5 oz (148 ml) pure maple syrup, plus extra if needed

1 cup (240 ml) unsweetened almond milk

1 tbsp (15 ml) vanilla

Pinch of sea salt

½ cup (85 g) strawberry wedges

2 tbsp (20 g) roughly chopped pistachios

Add the avocados, cacao, cinnamon, cayenne, syrup, almond milk, vanilla and salt to a blender. Blend until completely smooth. Taste for seasoning and sweetness, and add more cinnamon or maple syrup as necessary. Serve in a bowl and garnish with the strawberry wedges and pistachios.

NIEVE DE CAMOTE MORADO

(Purple Sweet Potato Ice Cream)

In my family, *camotes* (sweet potatoes) are usually eaten around the holiday season—cooked in raw sugar and cinnamon to create a candied camote dish. Sweet potatoes are very nutritious, with high amounts of fiber and vitamin A. They deserve to make their way onto our plate more often, even if it's in ice cream form!

In this recipe, we'll be making a simple ice cream base with a beautiful and vivid purple hue. You can make it your own by adding toasted nuts, a drop of lavender oil or diced fresh fruit—the choices are endless. It doesn't require an ice-cream maker, but if you already have one on hand, you can use the machine's operating instructions to create a creamier texture.

YIELD: 3-4 SERVINGS

2 large purple sweet potatoes

1 (14-oz [414-ml]) can full-fat coconut milk, refrigerated

½–¾ cup (120–180 ml) pure maple syrup

1 tbsp (15 ml) vanilla

1 tbsp (8 g) tapioca flour

1½ cups (360 ml) unsweetened coconut milk

Pinch of salt

Edible flowers, to garnish (optional)

Preheat the oven to 400°F (200°C).

Place the sweet potatoes on a baking sheet, and poke holes in them using a fork. Cover with foil and roast for about 1 hour until soft and tender. Allow the sweet potatoes to cool completely.

Add 1½ cups (300 g) of peeled sweet potato to a blender. Open the can of coconut milk and scoop out all the fat on the surface and any solid pieces floating in the coconut milk, and add to the blender. Add ½ cup (120 ml) of the maple syrup, vanilla, tapioca flour, unsweetened coconut milk and salt. Blend until smooth and creamy. Taste and add more maple syrup if needed. Add the ice cream base to a medium plastic container with a lid so the base is 2 to 3 inches (5 to 8 cm) high and place in the freezer for at least 3 hours.

Once the ice cream is set, you can use an ice cream scoop to make round ice-cream balls. Top with edible flowers, if desired.

NIEVE DE AGUACATE

(Avocado Ice Cream)

If you can't tell from this book so far, I really love avocados. You'll even see this versatile ingredient featured in a couple of recipes in the *bebidas* portion of this book. Avocados are the perfect intersection of flavors from rich, creamy, buttery and earthy. It's a fruit that has been grown and cultivated by indigenous people in Mexico as early as 500 B.C. It's been a staple in Mexican cuisine for generations, and is oftentimes a baby's first food.

For this recipe, we're blending fatty, nutrient-dense avocado flesh with coconut oil for a rich and decadent ice cream that will always hit the spot on a hot summer day. It's topped with a quick and easy raw cacao and coconut ganache and pistachio shavings. It doesn't require an ice cream maker, but if you already have one on hand, you can use the machine's operating instructions to create a creamier texture.

YIELD: 4 SERVINGS

For the Ice Cream

2 medium Hass avocados

⅓ cup (80 ml) pure maple syrup

1 tbsp (15 ml) vanilla

½ cup (120 ml) unsweetened almond milk

Pinch of salt

6 tbsp (90 ml) melted refined coconut oil

For the Chocolate Ganache

3 tbsp (21 g) raw cacao powder

3 tbsp (45 ml) melted refined coconut oil

3 tbsp (45 ml) pure maple syrup

1 tsp vanilla

For Serving

¼ cup (36 g) microplaned pistachios

To make the ice cream base, add the avocados, maple syrup, vanilla, almond milk and salt to a blender. Blend until smooth and creamy. Put the blender on low speed, and slowly pour in the coconut oil so it is evenly incorporated into the mixture. Add the ice cream base to a medium plastic container with a lid so the ice cream base is 2 to 3 inches (5 to 8 cm) high and place in the freezer for at least 3 hours.

To make the ganache, add the cacao, melted coconut oil, maple syrup and vanilla to a small bowl and whisk until completely smooth. If it hardens, place it over the stove or on a double boiler to loosen it up. Once the ice cream is set, you can use an ice-cream scoop to make round ice-cream balls. Use a spoon to pour the melted ganache over the ice cream. Top with pistachio shavings.

CHEF'S NOTE: Be sure to use refined coconut oil that does not smell or taste like coconut.

HIGOS CON QUESO

(Figs with Cheese)

My abuelitos lived in Canoga Park for many years after they migrated from their rancho in Zacatecas, Mexico. They brought that ranch style of living to LA's valley and used their backyard to plant sugarcane, corn, chiles and herbs and lemon, avocado, *huaje* and fig trees. My abuelito would climb into the fig tree, and all his grandchildren would gather to catch the sweet figs he tossed down to us. Figs remain a special treat that is near and dear to my heart. I love eating them fresh or preparing them in a simple recipe, like this one, where you still taste the natural and fresh flavors.

YIELD: 4–6 SERVINGS

For the Cream Cheese

1 cup (145 g) raw cashew pieces

¼ cup (60 ml) water, plus extra if needed

2–3 acidophilus probiotic capsules

1 tsp lemon juice, plus extra if needed

Salt, to taste

For the Candied Pepitas

2 tbsp (30 ml) maple syrup

2 tbsp (28 g) raw sugar

Pinch of salt

1 cup (138 g) pepitas

For the Figs

8 medium figs

¼ cup (60 ml) pure maple syrup, divided

To make the cream cheese, soak the cashews for 3 hours or overnight. Add the soaked and drained cashew pieces to a blender with the water, and blend until completely smooth. Scrape down the sides of the blender with a spatula to get any bits that didn't blend, and add more water if necessary to create a thick and creamy consistency. Once smooth, add the probiotic powder from the capsules and discard the casings. Pulse to incorporate the probiotic powder. Use a spatula to scrape the cream out of the blender and into a glass bowl. Cover the bowl with a cheesecloth, mesh bag or plastic wrap with holes poked into the surface. Allow the mixture to sit at room temperature and ferment for 15 to 18 hours, or until it is tangy and cheesy. Add the lemon juice and salt to the mixture and mix until fully incorporated. Taste for salt and lemon juice and add more as needed. Set aside.

To make the candied pepitas, preheat oven to 375°F (190°C).

Add the maple syrup, sugar and salt to a medium saucepan and heat over medium heat. Stir constantly until the sugar is melted and the mixture is slightly foamy. Add the pepitas and stir until they are fully coated. Lightly coat a medium baking sheet with oil, and spread the pepitas on the sheet. Bake for 10 minutes, stirring them halfway through. Remove the seeds from the oven and let them cool completely. You can stir the seeds occasionally while cooling to prevent them from sticking to the pan.

For the figs, preheat the oven broiler on high. Cut off the fig stems and make an X cut in the top of each fig until you get about halfway through each fig. Place the figs on a small baking sheet and drizzle them with 2 tablespoons (30 ml) of the maple syrup. Add them to the top oven rack, and broil for about 5 to 10 minutes, or until they look soft, slightly charred and release their juices. Take the figs out of the oven, and allow them to cool slightly until they are warm. Use 2 small spoons to add the cream cheese to the center of each fig. Drizzle them with the remaining maple syrup and garnish with the candied pepitas.

CAPIROTADA DE XOCOLATE
(Chocolate Bread Pudding)

One of my favorite desserts growing up was *capirotada*. My mom and abuelita made it when family was visiting or on chilly days. They each had similar recipes but gave it their own unique flavor with fruit choices or sprinkles to top it off. I'm continuing a family tradition, and adding my own vegan twist that includes chocolate.

For those of you who are not familiar with capirotada, it is a bread pudding dish usually eaten on Good Friday. Most recipes generally include *bolillo* or bread soaked in mulled syrup, and also includes nuts, seeds and sometimes fresh fruit. While some classic capirotada recipes ask for cheese, butter and white sugar, I opted for ingredients like shredded coconut and sliced almonds.

YIELD: 6-8 SERVINGS

3 wheat bolillo or birote (day-old bread) chopped into ½-inch (1.3-cm) dice

6 cups (1.4 L) unsweetened almond milk

½ cup (43 g) raw cacao powder

1 (7-oz [198-g]) piloncillo raw sugar cone

2 whole Mexican cinnamon sticks

3 whole cloves

2 bananas, divided

1 Gala apple, cored and quartered

1 tbsp (14 g) vegan butter (optional)

¼ cup (42 g) raisins

¼ cup (29 g) sliced almonds

¼ cup (16 g) shredded unsweetened toasted coconut

Turn the oven broiler on high. Layer the bread cubes on a baking sheet and place under the broiler for 1 to 2 minutes, or until the bread is toasted throughout. Remove from the oven and set aside to cool.

Pour the almond milk and cacao powder in a medium pot over medium heat. Whisk to fully incorporate the cacao. Add the piloncillo, cinnamon, cloves, 1 whole peeled banana and the apple. Bring to a boil, and then turn down to a simmer. Stir until the piloncillo has dissolved. Let it steep for 15 minutes with the heat off. Strain and pour the liquid back into the pot.

Grease a baking dish with vegan butter (if using). Line the bottom of the dish with a layer of the toasted bread. Pour ¼ of the liquid over the bread and cover with banana slices from the remaining banana and ⅓ of the raisins, almonds and coconut. Add another layer of bread and repeat the process. You should be able to fit 2 to 3 layers of bread. When the final layer of bread has been laid out, pour the remaining liquid on top and cover with the remaining raisins, almonds and coconut. Cover with aluminum foil and allow the capirotada to set in the refrigerator for at least 2 to 3 hours or overnight so the bread fully absorbs most of the liquid prior to baking.

Preheat the oven to 350°F (180°C). Allow the capirotada to come back to room temperature. Bake for 30 minutes, remove the foil, and bake for an additional 5 minutes to brown and crisp the top. Remove from the oven and let it rest for 20 minutes before serving.

CHEF'S NOTE: If you can't find piloncillo, you can use unrefined sugar as a substitute.

BEBIDAS

Drinks

Oftentimes, people treat drinks as an afterthought—just something to have alongside your meal. When I started Todo Verde back in 2015, I was at local farmers' markets with only a drink menu of superfood smoothies and agua fresca. I didn't want to be the afterthought drink that people purchased to pair with the food they purchased from other vendors at the market. I wanted to make a menu of items that people would crave and seek at the market.

After a few months at a new market, I had people hunting us down for a cup of our famous Amorcito Agua Fresca made with strawberry, rose, chia and maple syrup, or our Abuelita's Xocolate Caliente (page 147) made with raw cacao, dates, almond milk, cinnamon, vanilla, cayenne, sea salt and maple syrup. Soon after, people were asking if they could buy gallons to take home and drink throughout the week.

This chapter shares some of those special recipes that keep us opening the refrigerator to see if there is just one last cupful. These drink recipes are just as much a part of the meal as their savory counterparts. They make any meal extra special, and I hope you enjoy them as much as I do.

HORCHATA NEGRA CON CHIA
(Black Rice Horchata with Chia)

Horchata is a beverage that has traveled and transformed through generations, starting from its origin in West Africa. It was originally native to the people of Nigeria and Mali who used tiger nuts to create a milky, sweet, protein-rich staple. Through conquest and colonization, it later spread to Spain where white rice was used as the base and was spiced with Ceylon cinnamon native to Sri Lanka. This drink is now most popular in Mexico and Central America, where white rice continues to serve as its dense and milky base.

This recipe has surprised and shocked many of our Todo Verde clients who can't believe it can taste like *horchata* since we are leaving out the signature white hue. We opt for black rice, which you will see is actually purple when you blend it, and add activated charcoal for the onyx black version of this recipe that continues to evolve.

YIELD: 4 SERVINGS

½ cup (82 g) uncooked rinsed and drained black rice

6½ cups (1.6 L) water, divided

¾ cup (180 ml) pure maple syrup, plus extra if needed

1 tbsp (12 g) chia seeds

1 tbsp (15 ml) vanilla

1½ tbsp (9 g) ground Mexican cinnamon, plus extra if needed

1½ tbsp (8 g) activated charcoal

Add the rice and 5 cups (1.2 L) of the water to a bowl and allow the rice to soak for at least 2 hours and up to 24 hours.

In a pitcher or *vitrolero*, add the remaining water and syrup. Use a whisk to mix in the chia seeds, whisking as you pour them into the water so they don't stick together. Keep whisking until the chia seeds start to plump and absorb some of the water. Slowly whisk in the vanilla, cinnamon and activated charcoal. Set aside.

Add the soaked rice to a blender (in batches if needed) with some of the soaking liquid. Blend until the mixture is completely smooth. Pour the mixture into a fine strainer over the pitcher or vitrolero, and use a spoon to help the mixture move through the strainer. Add the remaining pulp in the strainer back into the blender, and blend with any more soaked rice and the soaking water. Blend again and strain into the pitcher or vitrolero. Add any remaining soaking water to the vitrolero. Taste for maple syrup and cinnamon and add more if needed.

Let your horchata sit in the refrigerator for 1 hour, or until it's fully chilled. Before serving, use a spoon or ladle to mix the horchata since the rice will settle at the bottom of the container, and pour over ice.

CHEF'S NOTE: The activated charcoal doesn't affect the flavor of the horchata; it only changes the color. The black rice is a milky purple when blended and doesn't make the horchata black without the charcoal. If you can't find the charcoal, you can still make the horchata without it.

AGUA FRESCA DE AGUACATE CON CHIA

(Avocado Agua Fresca with Chia)

I love creating unique flavors and textures with food. Whenever I mentioned that Todo Verde makes agua fresca, people assume that you make the traditional *aguas de jamaica*, white rice horchata and *tamarindo*. Those are all so delicious, but I wanted to make aguas that felt special and uniquely Todo Verde.

Avocado remains one of my all-time favorite ingredients. It's perfect with so many savory dishes, but it's rarely seen as an ingredient for a sweet recipe. Here, I'm pairing ripe avocados with fresh cucumber and tangy orange juice. The avocado gives this agua a creamy and slightly frothy consistency, and the cucumber and orange brighten it up.

YIELD: 4 SERVINGS

6½ cups (1.6 L) water, divided

¾ cup (180 ml) pure maple syrup, plus extra if needed

2 tbsp (23 g) chia seeds

1 medium Hass avocado

2 oz (57 g) Persian cucumber

½ cup (120 ml) orange juice

In a pitcher or vitrolero, add 1½ cups (360 ml) of the water and the maple syrup. Use a whisk to slowly mix in the chia seeds (so they don't stick together). Whisk until the chia seeds start to plump and absorb some of the water. Set aside.

Add the avocado and cucumber to a blender (in batches if needed) along with 3 cups (720 ml) of the water. Blend until the mixture is completely smooth. Pour the mixture into the pitcher or vitrolero. Add the orange juice and remaining water to the vitrolero and mix until fully incorporated. Taste for maple syrup and add more if needed.

Let the agua fresca sit in the refrigerator for 1 hour, or until it's fully chilled. Before serving, use a spoon or ladle to mix the agua fresca and pour over ice.

AGUA FRESCA DE TUNA CON SALVIA Y CHIA

(Prickly Pear and Sage Agua Fresca with Chia)

Tunas (not to be confused with tuna fish) or prickly pears are the juicy red fruit that grows on the edges of prickly pear cactus leaves. Their slightly spiky exterior is similar to other cactus leaves covered in thorns and spines, and their flesh is completely filled with small edible round seeds.

When we ate tunas growing up, we used a knife to cut off the stem side, then sliced a slit running from top to stem so we could peel the entire skin off the flesh with one swoop. We would bite down enough to break down the juicy and sweet flesh, but not hard enough to break down all the seeds—many times swallowing the tiny seeds whole. I've been warned by elders in my family that you shouldn't eat too many *tunas* (5 to 6!) in a day so the seeds can easily digest. Not too worry, this recipe removes the seeds so you can enjoy all the flavors of this succulent fruit.

YIELD: 4 SERVINGS

5 sage leaves, plus extra to garnish

4½ cups (1.1 L) water, divided

¾ cup (180 ml) pure maple syrup

2 tbsp (23 g) chia seeds

1½ lbs (680 g) tunas or prickly pears

Add the sage leaves to the bottom of a pitcher or vitrolero with a splash of water and a splash of maple syrup. Use the back of a wooden spoon to muddle the sage leaves so they release their flavor. Add 2 cups (480 ml) of the water to the pitcher or vitrolero to start the base. Slowly whisk in the chia seeds. Keep whisking until your chia seeds start to plump and absorb some of the water. Add the maple syrup.

Using tongs and a knife, cut the stem or base off each tuna. Cut a long slit from the top of the fruit to the base. Use your fingers and tongs to peel back the skin. Once you've removed the skins from all the tunas, add the tunas to a blender with the remaining water. Turn your blender on low. You want to break down the tunas while keeping the seeds as whole as possible. Once you've blended to a smooth consistency, add the mixture to a fine strainer over the pitcher or vitrolero. Use a spoon to help you move the mixture through the strainer. This will leave you with all the tuna juice and will remove the seeds.

Let the agua fresca sit in the refrigerator for 1 hour, or until it's fully chilled. Before serving, use a spoon or ladle to mix and pour over ice. Garnish each glass with a fresh sage leaf.

MEZCLA DE MICHELADA

(Michelada Mix)

Nothing says summertime in LA like a cold *michelada* on a Sunday afternoon along with a perfectly salted rim and a light Mexican beer. People have described micheladas as a Mexican Bloody Mary, but it is so much more than that—with its own distinct flavors of acid and spice. I like to argue that tomatoes are native Mexican ingredients and tomato-based drinks have been made by Mexicans for much longer than anyone else.

Legend has it that General Michel Ésper of San Luis Potosí would gather at a local bar and ask for ice, salt, lime and hot sauce to add to his *chelada* or beer. Others quickly started asking for this beer variation, and it was named michelada in his honor. Since then, the recipe has taken on many variations and has even included clam juice and anchovies to create a rich flavor. This recipe still gives your taste buds all the feels with a delicious balance of lemon, spice and savory tang to coat your tongue as you sing along to your favorite jams by the pool on a Sunday afternoon in LA.

YIELD: 4 SERVINGS

3 cups (720 ml) tomato juice

2 tbsp (30 ml) hot sauce such as Tapatío or Cholula

½ cup (120 ml) lemon juice

1 tbsp (15 ml) vegan Worcestershire sauce

2 tbsp (16 g) Tajín chile powder, plus extra to garnish

Salt, to taste

1 lemon, cut into wedges, to serve

4 light Mexican beers, to serve

Add the tomato juice, hot sauce, lemon juice, Worcestershire sauce, Tajín and salt to a pitcher and mix until fully incorporated. Taste for spice and salt level, and add more as needed.

Add extra Tajín or spiced salt (you can mix chile powder and salt) to a small shallow plate, and use a lemon wedge to moisten the rim of the beer glasses. Dip the rim of each glass into the Tajín or spiced salt. Fill the glass with ice and add the michelada mix until the glass is about half full. (I love the mix more than the beer, so I add quite a bit to my glass.) Top off the glass with a light Mexican beer and serve the remaining beer on the side.

CHEF'S NOTE: You can find vegan Worcestershire sauce online or at your local health food store.

ABUELITA'S XOCOLATE CALIENTE

(Hot Chocolate)

If you grew up in a Mexican household, you probably had Abuelita or Ibarra hot chocolate every time it rained and over the holidays. My favorite days growing up were staying home "sick" on rainy days, curling up on the couch to catch up on my favorite shows while dipping a bolillo or *birote* into a steaming hot mug of Abuelita. There was a perfect balance of chocolate and cinnamon with plenty of sugar . . . maybe a little too much sugar.

Cacao is a native ingredient that has been used for generations in Mexico and has elevated cuisine across the globe from Swiss chocolate techniques to Ecuadorian dark chocolate blends. *Xocolatl* is a Nahuatl word that translates to "bitter water" or "drink." The cacao bean began being processed by the Mayan people, who figured out that this sacred bean needed to undergo a process of fermenting, drying and roasting the seeds and then removing the cacao nibs from the shells to be ground into a cacao paste or powder. It was inevitable that a huge corporation like Nestlé would use cacao to create a sugary, spiced chocolate recipe that is marketed to Mexican communities as if it was their own abuelita's recipe.

This homemade version leaves out all the highly processed ingredients and focuses on the cacao and cinnamon flavors with a little kick of heat using cayenne pepper as an option. The dates make this *xocolate* recipe slightly creamy and frothy. If you have a *molinillo* on hand, you can use it to create a frothy chocolate. To use the molinillo, place the handle between your palms and roll it back and forth quickly like you are rubbing your palms together. This action aerates the milk, which makes it frothy, and it takes some time and effort that you won't regret.

YIELD: 4 SERVINGS

¾ cup (122 g) pitted dates

6½ cups (1.6 L) unsweetened almond milk

⅓ cup (36 g) raw cacao powder

Pinch of cayenne (optional)

1 tbsp (8 g) Mexican cinnamon powder

⅓ cup (80 ml) pure maple syrup

1 tsp vanilla

Pinch of sea salt

Place the dates in a bowl of hot water to fully submerge the dates. Let them soak for about 10 minutes, and strain them to remove the water. They should be plump and juicy.

Add the dates and almond milk to a blender, and blend until completely smooth. Add the mixture to a medium pot, turn on the burner to medium-low and add the cacao powder, cayenne (if using), cinnamon, maple syrup, vanilla and salt. Whisk to combine until fully incorporated. This may take a little time, since the cacao tends to stay on the surface until fully worked into the mixture. Bring the mixture to a simmer and continue to whisk or use a molinillo to create a frothy xocolatl caliente.

LICUADO DE CACAO Y AVENA
(Cacao and Oats Smoothie)

If you didn't know this already, I love smoothies. When I first started Todo Verde, it was at local farmers' markets throughout Los Angeles, making superfood smoothies and agua fresca with ingredients from the farmers at the market like kale, strawberries, stone fruit, apples, herbs, berries and even tomatoes to make an Ecuadorian-style agua fresca. Unfortunately the world—outside of Ecuador—wasn't ready for that one yet!

Smoothies are a great way to experiment with flavor combinations, density and color. I usually reach for a smoothie once a day. Sometimes they are quick and easy meal replacements, and other times they serve as an in-between meal snack. Here is Todo Verde's classic Brown Power smoothie recipe using raw cacao, oats, banana and kale for a nostalgic *chocomil*-esque morning pick-me-up or a chocolate dessert stand-in. If you don't have raw cacao or kale, use other fresh ingredients you already have at home, such as dark chocolate and spinach. Have fun experimenting!

YIELD: 1-2 SERVINGS

1 large banana, peeled

1 large kale leaf

2 tbsp (12 g) cacao powder

3 tbsp (21 g) whole oats

1 tsp vanilla

3 pitted dates

1½ cups (360 ml) unsweetened almond milk

½ cup (70 g) ice

Cacao nibs, to garnish (optional)

Add the banana, kale, cacao, oats, vanilla, dates, almond milk and ice to a blender and blend until smooth and creamy. If you have cacao nibs on hand, add them to the top as a garnish for a little bite while you sip on your smoothie.

LICUADO DE AGUACATE

(Avocado Smoothie)

Growing up, avocado was mostly identified as an ingredient you used in savory dishes. We ate the creamy, oily-green flesh in ceviche, tacos, salsas and as a finishing touch on most dishes. It wasn't until I ventured throughout South America that I noticed folks in Ecuador and Peru using them as an ingredient in sweet dishes like a *batido de aguacate* or avocado smoothie.

This recipe is a nod to my Ecuadorian and Mexican roots, and the batidos de aguacate throughout Latino America along with the chia seeds of Mexico and Guatemala. It's a light smoothie that's perfect for a hot summer day where you want something refreshing and filling. It has notes of fresh citrus and earthy kale. Top it with chia seeds for a little crunch, and you have all the essentials to keep you going until your next delicious meal.

YIELD: 1-2 SERVINGS

1 large orange, peeled

1 large kale leaf

¼ medium Hass avocado

1 large banana, peeled

½ cup (70 g) ice

1 tbsp (12 g) chia seeds, plus extra to garnish

Add the orange to the blender first as it will help break down the other ingredients when it blends. Add the kale, avocado, banana, ice and chia seeds. Blend until creamy and smooth. Pour into a glass, and top with chia seeds to garnish.

INGREDIENT
SOURCES

Many of the ingredients needed to put together these recipes can be found at grocery stores and *tortillerias* in Mexican neighborhoods. A Mexican grocery store will be a huge source for dried chiles, spices, herbs and ripe produce. You can typically track down harder to find items like dethorned nopales and prickly pears. Some larger stores oftentimes carry prepared masa for tortillas and tamales, although I still recommend making your masa from organic masa harina. Local tortillerias will also have prepared masa for tortillas and tamales along with already made and packaged tortillas. This is great if you're in a pinch and need to prepare something quickly. Keep in mind that most grocery stores and tortillerias use lard in their *masa preparada* for tamales.

You'll also source many ingredients from your local health food stores and farmers' markets if you have any in your area. Health food stores are a great source for organic items and brands such as Bob's Red Mill, Bragg, Native Forest and Follow Your Heart. Items like the acidophilus will be found in the refrigerated supplements section. Farmers' markets are the best source for locally grown, great quality fresh produce.

If you're not able to find some ingredients, you can also find a wide variety of items online.

Bob's Red Mill

bobsredmill.com
Organic masa harina, corn flour, tapioca flour, oat flour, nutritional yeast

Diaspora Co.

diasporaco.com
Turmeric

Follow Your Heart

followyourheart.com
Egg replacer, vegan mayonnaise

Gold Mine Natural Foods

shop.goldminenaturalfoods.com
Organic masa harina, blue corn, pepitas, beans, quinoa, nori, sesame seeds, brown rice

Kernel of Truth Organics

instagram.com/kerneloftruthorganics
Organic blue and yellow nixtamal, masa and tortillas, based in Los Angeles

Lucky Vitamin

luckyvitamin.com
Jackfruit, agar, pure maple syrup, black rice, cacao, activated charcoal, liquid aminos, brown rice, flax seeds, chia seeds, hemp hearts, coconut milk, coconut cream, vegan Worcestershire sauce

Masienda

masienda.com
Organic masa harina, dried corn, cal

Mex Grocer

mexgrocer.com
Chiles, spices, huitlacoche (cuitlacoche), dried epazote, corn husks, hibiscus, achiote (annatto) paste, chile California, chile de arbol, chipotle en adobo, chipotle morita, chile guajillo, chile ancho, sesame seeds, tamarind, Mexican cinnamon, piloncillo, nutmeg, Tajín, saladitos, hot sauce, beans, chia seeds, tostadas, tortilla chips, tortilla press, molcajete, tamale steamer

Native Seeds

nativeseeds.org
Organic dried nixtamalized pozole, mayocoba beans, pinto beans, black beans, chile de arbol, chipotle morita, chile guajillo, chile ancho, spices

Olive Nation

olivenation.com
Rose water, huitlacoche, black rice, brown rice, chia seeds, hemp hearts, dates

Thrive Market

thrivemarket.com
Jackfruit, heart of palm, raw cashew pieces, almonds, pepitas, nutritional yeast, pure maple syrup, black rice, refined coconut oil, quinoa, kelp granules, vegan mayonnaise, nori, cacao, activated charcoal, liquid aminos, brown rice, acidophilus (shipped in cold pack), flaxseeds, chia seeds, hemp hearts, coconut milk, coconut cream, vegan Worcestershire sauce, dates

ACKNOWLEDGMENTS

This book would not be possible without my ancestors, both known and unknown. They have shaped the culture of native food and have evolved through colonization, creating the unique cuisine of Mexico today. I am grateful for their endurance in the face of painful change and resilience to make things undoubtedly Mexican.

Abuelita Beatriz Del Real Alvarez y Abuelito Jesus Alvarez, les agradezco por guiar a nuestra familia a Los Ángeles y por mantenernos enraizados en la cultura de Monte Escobedo, Zacatecas.

Mom y Dad, gracias por enseñarme a trabajar duro y luchar por mis sueños. Les agradezco por siempre apoyarme y seguir conmigo en los buenos y malos momentos. Los quiero mucho y espero que les haga sentir orgullosos.

Rudy, I'm so grateful to have a partner who not only supports my dreams but does everything in his power to help me reach my goals. Your work constantly inspires me, and I hope to be as great of a support system to you. Te quiero forever.

Juan Carlos, Marcie, Amanda and Dominick, thank you for cooking with me in the kitchen every holiday and family party, taste testing the good and disastrous recipes and washing too many dishes to count.

Todo Verde Team, to those who are still with me and those who have moved on to different chapters of your lives, I thank you for building with me and for all your hard work.

Todo Verde Community, you have really been an incredible force that makes me feel like I have to keep going.

Claudia Serrato, your decolonial food work is what inspired me to become plant-based years ago, and you've continued to teach me so much in such a short time. Thank you for being a femtor as well as a wealth of knowledge.

Friends and recipe testers, thank you for all your feedback, for eating the good and bad batches and for supporting me on this delicious journey.

Cindi and Zach, you've seen something in me since day one that I still have trouble seeing most days. You have believed in me and given me space to show others that plant-based food is actually pretty damn delicious.

Zohra, thank you for your friendship, photographic vision and for making our food look so delicious.

Page Street Team, thank you for seeing something special in me and for your incredible patience.

You, the readers, thank you for trusting me in your kitchen.

To all these named above, and many more who have helped along this journey, I thank you.

ABOUT THE AUTHOR

Todo Verde founder, Jocelyn Ramirez, is a plant-based chef, college professor, yoga instructor and advocate for healthy food access in her community. After Jocelyn's father was diagnosed with cancer for the second time, she created a plant-based superfood smoothie diet that made him dramatically stronger and helped with a quick recovery. As she drove across Los Angeles in search of healthy food options, she was astounded by the lack of access to good food in her neighborhood.

Jocelyn founded Todo Verde in 2015 with a mission to create delicious and healthy plant-based food inspired by her Mexican and South American roots for the Eastside community of LA. She left her career in higher education to pursue a new path in foodways related to culture and tradition and references traditional recipes passed down for generations within her family. As she continues to learn about the health benefits of nutrient-dense foods and healthy ecosystems, she offers knowledge on healthy living with the community through workshops, dialogues, food demonstrations and speaking engagements in relation to critical analysis of the industrial food system and traditional foodways.

Jocelyn's background includes degrees in Fine Art, Design and Business and she has also trained at the Matthew Kenney Culinary Academy. Her work has been featured in several press outlets including the *Los Angeles Times*, *Los Angeles Magazine*, Munchies Food by Vice, Spotify, BuzzFeed, *Smithsonian*, mitú, and more. In 2017, Jocelyn cofounded Across Our Kitchen Tables, an organization focused on uplifting women of color in the food industry. It hosts skillshares and an annual symposium. She currently sits on the Culinary Advisory Board for Food Forward and the Leadership Circle for the Los Angeles Food Policy Council.

@la_yoselin
@todoverde

INDEX